Think on These Things

Thoughts are things. Left unguarded we can expect them to rule us with ruthless persistence. Like attracts like. We are what we think.

Emerson believed there was something stronger than any material force. It was his belief that thought rules the world. To think positively is sometimes referred to as refusing to face reality. But who is wise enough to determine what reality is, and who can describe it? The things we see and touch are merely objects made up of tiny particles we can't see individually. So it is with reality—tiny thoughts we don't remember thinking, but the result is obviously positive or negative.

If we think continually of how sick and nervous, how unhappy and poverty-stricken we are, then we can expect to be so afflicted. Tiny thoughts produce large results. When we've learned to control our thinking, then we have a chance to control our circumstances.

Imperfect thoughts, like unsavory characters, can come to anyone's door, but we don't have to let them in. Sometimes we have to look beyond present appearances and see the truth of things, to know that any product is worth only as much as the quality of its material. Sometimes we would be wise to put into practice the teaching of Philippians 4:8:

"Whatsoever things are true, whatsoever things are honest, whatsoever things are just, whatsoever things are pure, whatsoever things are lovely, whatsoever things are of good report: if there be any virtue, and if there be any praise . . . think on these things."

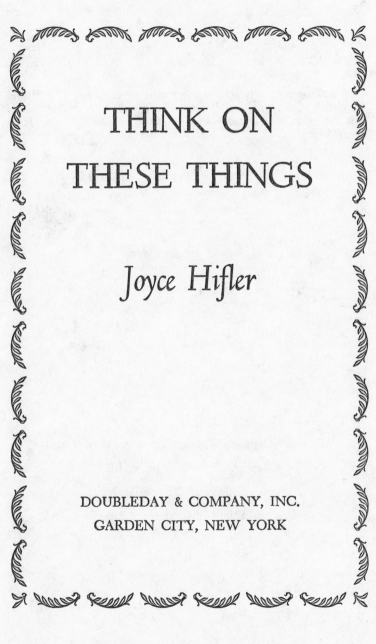

THINK ON THESE THINGS

Joyce Hifler

DOUBLEDAY & COMPANY, INC.
GARDEN CITY, NEW YORK

The author wishes to acknowledge with appreciation The World Publishing Company and Executive Editor Sid Steen for use of this collection of columns which originally appeared in the *Tulsa Daily World*.

To my daughter Jane

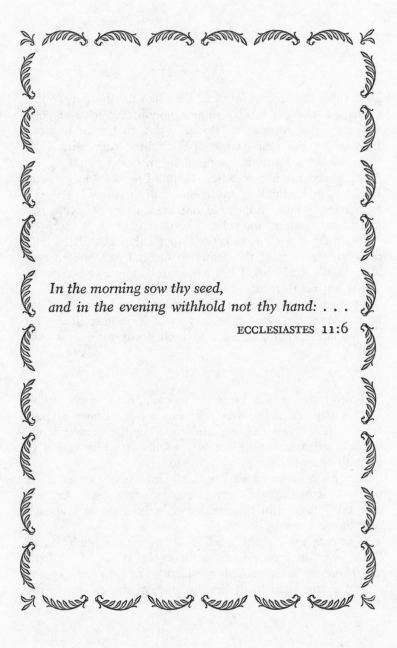

In the morning sow thy seed,
and in the evening withhold not thy hand: . . .

ECCLESIASTES 11:6

In the frantic search for something that has meaning to life, we have a tendency to do a thing simply because everyone else is doing it. It becomes a "thing," a fad that must be done to keep on the inside circle. There's little originality, little thought, but a lot of following along in beaten paths.

It is a mistaken idea to believe that all I see with my eyes and the limits of my thinking are the limits of the world. There is a tremendously interesting world out there never before investigated, and I am an individual like no one else.

It is quite marvelous to break through the shell of the middling and to discover the ability to see and feel, and to hear more keenly. Suddenly, I can feel more kindly, not because of who I am on this earth, but because I'm a child of God.

I can see more color, more light, more vision because I'm not being shown, I'm discovering. My world is no longer based on passing fancies, but on the lasting built slowly within me, with love.

To so many, getting up in the morning is the worst way to begin a day. To them every morning is the morning after, a time to feel nervous anxiety and regret in the deepest sense, while to others morning is a new world. Yesterday ceased to be with sleep last night.

How much better off we'd be if only for a few hours we could put out of our minds every painful thought and every unpleasant person until the mind and body could find enough new life to begin again.

"The early morning hath gold in its mouth," wrote Franklin. But it has things more precious than gold. It has life as fresh and sweet as the shimmering, clinging dewdrops in the first rays of golden sunlight. It has the grace of mimosa leaves rippling in the gentlest breeze. It has the gay songs of the birds and the love of a new awakening.

And in this breathless creation is something more. A new opportunity, another chance, a challenge to walk on, more strong, more forgiving, more loving.

Sleep deep and rest sweet, but rise glad. Don't let one joyful second be lost in dead oblivion. This is a vision of newness awaiting even the least to arise and accept the best—a new beginning.

Morning need not be a jury trial for oneself. Dawn and sleep can be a miraculous cleansing to set us out on our feet ready to begin again and in a friendlier atmosphere. We must feel friendly toward ourselves before we can possibly find morning good to anyone else.

Thomas Blake wrote: "Every morning lean thine arms awhile upon the window sill of heaven, and gaze upon thy Lord, then, with the vision in thy heart, turn strong to meet thy day."

We need to be strong to meet the day with self control, to find our reason and purpose, but, more important, to leave behind us the heavy and darkened thoughts that kept us from seeing the breath-taking beauty of the most important time— this morning.

There are very few days when we have control of our time. No matter what our schedule may be, there is always a change taking place that keeps something from happening when it is supposed to happen. And when the day is ended and the schedule has not been met, then it begins to drag on our spirits.

Soon we become so wound up in the problems of the moment that the delights of our souls drift away and become a part of the mist of "someday." Someday I will get to do what I want to do. Someday when this necessary work is finished— and is it possible that the things we believe to be so necessary are really robbers of our lives? Do we spend too much time with

3

the menial tasks and allow our creativity—the ability to bring newness into our lives—to dry up and become nonexistent?

William Blake called this creativity in man "God." One of the greatest poets ever to live, he believed that if man kept alive his ability to see and feel the beauty of life, his menial tasks would become easy and the way successful.

Yesterday is only a dream, tomorrow only a vision, but to-day—today we live. If we live as we should, our yesterdays will be dreams of happiness, and our tomorrows will be visions of hope.

Nothing is so sad as the man who spends all his time today judging tomorrow by his experiences of yesterday. He has a vision, but his faith does not support him to pursue it. If some great stroke of good fortune should overtake him, he will be all ready to go, but he doesn't really expect it to happen. So today he sits waiting for the world to change for him, never once guessing that he is the one who must change.

No one is so misled as the woman who has such a busy schedule that she hasn't time to listen to her children. She expects to take the time to play with them—someday. But it is today that the bridges must be built from the soul to the body to the spirit. It isn't something built from a quick kiss or a smart smack in the right place, but from daily communion and understanding.

Today is the very life of life when the best things are nearest —breath in our nostrils, light in our eyes, flowers at our feet, duties at our hand, and the path of God before us.

So you missed an opportunity! And they say that opportunity knocks only once—but, only if you believe it! Opportunity has been known to pound on the door and go unnoticed, and it has been known to whisper and be heard. It is all according to how hard we require opportunity to knock before we recognize it.

Our awareness of opportunity will reveal to us how many times it presents itself; so subtle, it may not be recognized by

4

How presumptuous of man to believe he owns one thing of lasting value that does not come from God.

Man must win his own heart before he can find happiness with others.

EMPLOYEE NO.	EMPLOYEE NAME		SHIFT	DEPT	DATE
560753	C B WEBB		2	8711	10-15-86

BLOOD DONOR CARD

PLEASE PRESENT THIS CARD TO THE RED CROSS REPRESENTATIVE
AT THE BLOOD BANK WHEN YOU DONATE

The blood you give helps you, your fellow-employees and your community. It forms a bank
from which you and your immediate family can draw in time of need.

GIVE A PINT OF BLOOD AND HELP SAVE A LIFE

IF YOU OR A MEMBER OF YOUR IMMEDIATE FAMILY NEEDS BLOOD, OR IF YOU
HAVE ANY QUESTIONS, CALL EMPLOYEE SERVICE.

☐ I CANNOT DONATE AT ANY TIME BECAUSE

SIGNED

(By our deeds we saved our minds)

NECC/ATA-1882

LOCKHEED ★

GA FORM 8590-2

LOCKHEED-GA. CO.

the casual eye. And usually it seems to be completely unprofitable to us personally. More often than not it is service to others without thought of return. It is humility, a willingness to accept the most humble beginnings. It is joy in finding communication with others and finding a kinship with them.

Have you heard of an opportunity fund? Some call it saving for a rainy day. Rainy days can be lovely, too. A rainy day can be an opportunity to get things done. But an opportunity can be any day, rain or shine.

Do you often have the opportunity to speak to your neighbor? It seems to happen too infrequently these days.

The most fun we can have comes when we've the opportunity to squelch an ugly rumor. You know, "curst be the tongue whence slanderous rumor, withering friendship's faith . . ." Sometimes a little friendship does wither, but if it really amounts to anything it will survive.

What a splendid opportunity to sit quietly and mentally forgive with such depth and joy as to start life anew. There is no greater blessing, no greater opportunity fund.

American editor A. E. Dunning writes, "Great opportunities come to all, but many do not know they have met them. The only preparation to take advantage of them, is simple fidelity to what each day brings."

A missed opportunity may well be another opportunity to prepare for a bigger and better one!

Haven't you heard someone say after experiencing something either good or bad, "I knew it was going to be that way." And perhaps the conviction was very strong that certain conditions would take a definite turn. But much of the time we say it not out of conviction, but resignedly, agreeing beforehand that something will be a certain way, and usually with dire overtones.

It used to be believed that we had no power to control anything coming to us. We were mere victims of circumstances, almost like stones waiting to be kicked aside. But we were taught, "As a man thinketh in his heart, so he is."

We must not be so presumptuous as to believe we know everything there is to know about the workings of the mind. But we attract a great many of our problems simply by dwelling on them in our thoughts.

Premonition, or "knowing" things are going to be a certain way, is merely giving us a little time to head off the trouble. Such things should be a challenge, not an accepted rule. "Know" better until you believe it into conviction and into being.

First things and first times . . . the newness of the present moment holds such a breath of youth, such a challenge. There are moments in everyone's life they wish they could relive. Just to recall those times when the newness, the memory of first things were beautiful and bewitching.

But life never stands still. It moves forward or it decays. It cannot hold on to the past in any way. If the newness of first things have not grown into finer and more beautiful moments, then it cannot go on.

Everyone can recall something so dear that it becomes new again just by thinking about it. Courage, love, joy, contentment, all these can call to mind the special moments that were beginnings of new eras, new times in living. The scales of life tip this way and that to make those times full of meaning and sometimes vividly painful. And then sometimes it takes a season to mend the heart and spirit. When they are ready, the experience of new times and new beginnings and first things will bloom once more and the youthful challenge again enchants.

We have often heard it said that God never closes one door unless he opens another. It is a great comfort to know we never

6

really lose when we believe, for any defeat can be turned to good if we will absorb the lesson in it.

And yet, how often we refuse to go through that door that has been opened for us. It is so much easier to stand back and wail about the closed one. There seems to be a certain amount of glorification in defeat. It is a subtle something that hides in man and keeps him from doing well that which he knows he is capable of doing. If he shows strength, he is afraid he will have to stand alone.

Sometimes a door will close for us because that particular one would have caused us more unhappiness, but it never closes for punishment. God is love and love does not punish, nor does it have any power but to give what is right and good for us. With this knowledge, we can by grace walk through those doors that open to us and know it is right.

Good ideas are the flowers of the mind, waiting to bloom for the benefit of the thinker.

We are constantly in the process of manufacturing ideas. Every waking moment we are thinking continually, making mental images of that which we desire or need. Everything we see was first an idea in someone's mind.

Ideas are fleeting messages that pass rapidly through the mind. Some of them are strong enough to impress the thinker. Many are not worth saving, but a few are very precious. They have to be sifted, sorted and analyzed for value. Then, they must be acted on immediately, for they are very perishable. Once we lose an idea, it is seldom if ever recaptured.

Everyone has access to a better and happier life through ideas, if we can trust the Divine Mind to give us the will and courage to follow through on them.

James Russell Lowell once wrote, "No man is born into the world whose work is not born with him." Each of us has been given a talent. It may not be some great shining thing that will attract attention and cause fame. But living has become so intricate, so great in detail, so fine in its workings, that it requires the skills of all men.

Every time we touch something, hear, see and feel, we are using the results of other people's talents. Too many think of their abilities to do certain things as just "another job." But that isn't true, because no matter how small your part may seem, it takes its place in the world of living as important and necessary as the greatest talent.

The secret of a successful talent is in its use. The most minute gift was put there for a purpose and we should never belittle it but gratefully devote our attention to developing its perfection.

There are a number of self-improvement books on the market today. Among them are excellent etiquette books teaching us the correct way of doing things and how to live more graciously with our fellow man. But one can be quite learned and lose the benefit of keeping the social graces with oneself.

You owe it to yourself to quit belittling your abilities in thought or word.

Self-respect is another necessity in order to keep on good terms with oneself.

You owe yourself spiritual growth—the ability to enter a church reverently and to sit quietly in your own preparatory service before the formal service begins.

It is your duty to fill your mind with the better thoughts, the sweetening of the nature and a measure of tolerance—for you will make mistakes, but there should also be the power to forgive oneself, to go on from there.

To be on good terms with oneself is to worry less about violating the rules of good behavior with all others.

Leave yourself a choice. It is a sorry state of affairs when a person's life becomes so regimented that it is impossible to make even one change in plans. There is a story about a gentleman who kept a record in minute detail of his living and every cent he earned so that he could make a trip abroad. The record keeping became such an obsession that when he could make the trip he took along crackers to keep from eating in the dining room aboard ship. The journey was nearly over before he discovered the price of his meals was included in the fare.

How much do we miss by refusing to accept the bounty of choices. "If only" and "I wish" are so over used. We bind ourselves daily by refusing to recognize the volume of opportunities open to each of us. All of life is not free, but there is much available for our personal selection.

Dr. William S. Sadler wrote of a woman who was so orderly and systematic in her living that she inquired of her minister how to go about dying since she had never done it before. Living in a systematic world is possible, but there are limits to what we can prepare for and about which to be orderly. Daily we meet and settle many small emergencies, and some not so small. And it is our developed ability to meet these things successfully and on the spur of the moment that makes a well-rounded individual.

But the steady, uniform methods of doing things does not necessarily mean a person is ready to meet every situation in life. In fact, such living often makes change practically impossible when change is sorely needed.

Order is heaven's first law. But order means first things first. A place for everything and everything in its place. Then, if we've learned how to live, we never have to worry about the art of dying gracefully.

What is it that keeps us from doing the creative things we want to do? Fear of venturing and losing, fear of the unknown. And yet, every day of our lives we venture and seldom acknowledge the fact that we didn't lose. We too often accomplish something because circumstances forced a courage we could not muster from mere desire.

Frequently we must simply have the audacity to lay aside the

9

taboos we have built for ourselves, for fear of appearing foolish, and follow a creative curiosity.

Robert Louis Stevenson wrote, "Give me a young man with brains enough to make a fool of himself." And he didn't mean intentionally acting foolishly, but that his fearlessness of appearing foolish enabled him to step outside the realms of what others would call the limits.

The simplest ventures often bring joy to many, particularly to the one who in the beginning dared to stand on his own chances of winning or losing.

This is a day that God has made, rejoice and be glad in it.

What we do with each day is largely decided by the thought we give it in the beginning and how we start a new day plays an immense part in the success or failure of either carefully laid plans, or helter-skelter activity.

We should open this day with as much reverence as if it were gift wrapped and presented to us personally, which it is.

What wonderful thing can I do this day that no one else could do! Shall I spend these precious moments complaining? Shall I sit glum at my work to make others feel morbid? Should I continually acknowledge how little I have and how badly I feel?

Or should I speak kindly, think kindly, feel kindly, and be so grateful that I have another opportunity today to do something for someone that will bring him joy and lift his spirits?

This day is in your hands. You will reap from it after the seeds which you plant. If you would be loved, then be lovable; if you want peace, be peaceable; and if you would ask freedom, grant freedom. And learn to forgive without reservation.

What is the texture of life?

Texture is that finely woven fabric of life that demands we have a congenial environment. It asks that we be industrious toward success, and that we should have a way of life, a purpose. We should hear the music of life and taste the bitter and the sweet.

Texture requires us to research every experience and learn the lesson in it. It orders us to communicate with life and make discoveries about ourselves and progress toward a texture where the coarse has been refined.

Frequently we should examine the texture of life to identify the quality. How wide is my world? How high is my sky?

All of us should know the "feel" of our own makeup, our capabilities, our gifts with which we have been divinely endowed. And we should think long on these words from Edna St. Vincent Millay's "Renascence":

"The world stands out on either side no wider than the heart is wide. Above the world is stretched the sky, no higher than the soul is high."

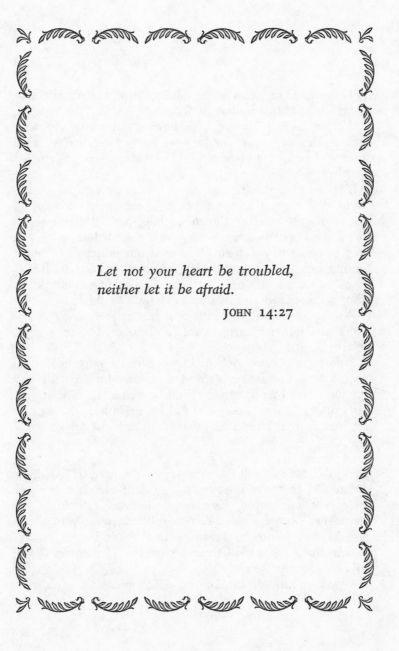

Let not your heart be troubled,
neither let it be afraid.

JOHN 14:27

There are many fears in the mind of man, but none so subtle, yet so effectual as fear of failure.

We are so afraid we've been unwise and wasted valuable time and it makes us wonder how many times we've failed those who depended upon us, and how many times we've failed ourselves.

It is easy to look back and see the places we would have different if it were still in our power. Time seems so short to make up and overcome the things long past. It seems sometimes that opportunities are there and gone before we've had time to make use of them. We condemn ourselves so much for the lack of knowledge when we most needed it. But if decisions were made on afterthought, they might not be as wise as those made quickly, without time to think.

We should no longer think about past failures, nor give undue thought to our chances for future ones, but only begin now to do the very best we can.

True failures come only to those who stop trying, for no age, no time, no place can stop the person who decides to try one more time. As Frederick William Farrar, English author, has written, "There is only one real failure in life that is possible, and that is, not to be true to the best one knows."

Where there's a will there's a way, it is written. If a desire is sincere and the results are for the good of everyone, the first giant steps have already been taken. American clergyman Joel Hawes has been quoted, "You may be whatever you resolve to be. Determine to be something in the world, and you will be something—'I cannot' never accomplishes anything; 'I will try' has wrought wonders."

A positive attitude can be one of the greatest joys to experience. To begin a day by willing everything good, and meeting any obstacle with the idea that it has no power, can make some of the most sudden and drastic changes in anyone's life.

To be something or someone is one of the strongest desires, but it does mean sacrifices of doubt and apprehension and feeling sorry for oneself. It means standing straighter when it is more comfortable to crawl. It means laughing instead of lamenting. It means thinking positively and speaking good words.

It is said that a great deal of talent is lost in this world for the want of a little courage. We often think of courage as the kind that wins wars and braves new fronts. But there is another plain, ordinary kind of courage that helps us face our everyday problems.

There is a surprising lack of this kind of courage, and it leads us to seek ways to dodge our responsibilities. It takes a tremendous amount of courage to face everything and everyone and take a firm stand for what we believe in. It takes courage to admit we have weaknesses and needs that we must overcome. It is a daily fight to follow the right road when the wrong one looks so smooth. And it takes courage to believe, when obstacles face us.

God must see a bit of courage in each of us, for strength to overcome is available to all who are courageous in asking for help to be courageous.

Sensibility is said to be neither good nor evil in itself, but in its application. Sometimes we just "out-sensible" ourselves. In the course of years we come to see the pattern of the truly sensible. What have we at this moment that really means anything? Does it give us happiness? Did it once seem most impractical? Was it worth fighting for?

The intellectual strives for knowledge and in his absorption leaves the world but hardly leaves a vacancy. The materialistic must have everything at the price of peace, and his possessions decay but never his chaotic soul. And the insecure forfeits the most minute comforts to save for that rainy day. Happiness would have been greater and far more lasting if the fund had been smaller and used as an opportunity fund.

The fine line of sensibility can be most elusive, but it seems to be more clearly seen when we relax and quit shoving to get there. If the place we desire is meant for us, it will come when we learn the way isn't always sharp and direct and by demand.

Life equips us in many ways for very special purposes. Some never catch the high vision as to why they are the objects of ridicule or are the witnesses of cruelty—while others bear the brunt of many heartaches and still are capable of knowing compassion for those who cause it.

Jesus was such a man—He withstood more than we are able to comprehend, but He asked that His tormentors be forgiven for they knew not what they were doing.

It is our individual decision whether we choose to be one of the throng of agitators who see only to confirm what everyone else is doing, or we can catch the vision of greater things and walk firmly in paths we believe are right.

To fall into the role of just another face in the crowd is an ill-chosen path, but to lead others to follow is the essence of parasitism—the need to have others be just as nameless and even more dependent.

"There is no royal road to anything—One thing at a time, and all things in succession. That which grows slowly endures" —J. G. Holland.

The first lesson we have to learn is that instant success in anything is a fantasy. The overnight success stories we hear about are really products of much preparation.

If we could view a life laid out before us, we could see it is much like a hand sewn quilt, built of many tiny pieces, colors of every hue, fabrics of every kind, and patiently joined together by tiny stitches to give many years of service. Maybe we missed a stitch someplace and it caused a weak place, but the strength of many other stitches will carry it through. Finally a complete quilt has been created and it is strong and lasting.

When we truly want to move ahead we build our lives a quilt block at a time, patiently adding to another part of life until we have the strength and courage to endure.

Take one step at a time, but take it positively forward! The patience will be rewarded. To have a dream come true we must first have a dream. Don't look back. The past is gone, but the future is still in our hands.

It has been written that an optimist is someone who can fall ten stories and call out to each floor in passing that everything is okay so far. It has also been said that an optimist is someone who refuses to see things as they really are.

It is far better, the pessimist believes, to look for the worst so as to be pleasantly surprised when things are better than expected. Then, if they are as bad as he thought they would be he won't be so disappointed.

But this is somewhat like backing into a room so to avoid seeing the beauty of it only to find it was an elevator shaft.

There can be no advancement where men expect the worst and believe that going outside the limits of ordinary thinking is only day dreaming. Thinkers, capable of forecasting and predicting answers before the questions happen, are in great demand.

Only the optimist can fill the bill. Only he can dare to believe there are things waiting for discovery and further development.

An optimist questions life the same as a pessimist, but the difference is that he knows there is an answer and also knows he will find it. He is aware that the cherries that life is supposed to be a bowl of have pits, but he is prepared to remove them. His mind does not dwell on the pits, but on the sweetness of the cherries.

There will be situations that will make us afraid. Fear is a common sense emotion that keeps us from walking in front of a moving car or from jumping off the deep end of anything. And there are periods of natural anxiety when we want too much to perform well, and the butterflies begin to flutter.

Then, there is another kind of fear that is unnatural. It has the ability to possess us and rule over our very lives. It is that "what if" fear that builds nests in our minds and hatches dire images that scare the daylights out of us. It can keep the lights off, the doors bolted, and the windows of our souls locked against the most beautiful things in life.

It is no disgrace in this day to ask for professional help in understanding our fears. Only the very foolish would consider this help a crutch. It is a brave person who admits the need for help and has the courage to go and find it.

They are the pioneers in recognizing our existence as three-fold: mental, physical . . . and spiritual.

How weak-willed we are at times when we've made a decision and know we must stand on it. It is so much easier to give in to the easy way of doing things.

We are almost a "house divided against itself," and the strain of staying with a decision seems almost our enemy. But no one ever gained much stature by giving in to oneself against better judgment. And no one ever gets anywhere by scattering his efforts.

Making a decision is difficult enough without losing one's determination in following through. Laying down the responsibility is somewhat like warning a child to behave himself and then permitting him to continue to misbehave.

How long has it been since you've proven to yourself that you mean business in carrying out a plan?

A man of wisdom has written that we have firmness of character when we have the ability to say "no" to the wrong as well as to those things which are good but stand in the way of our progress.

Always remember that to want something that is good *and*

right is the blessing. God gave us the ability to desire or we would never have thought of using it. But He also gave us the ability to cry, to feel pain and the freedom to choose whether we go on or quit.

In our lives we face many decisions. Some are hard to make because we know we must turn our backs upon something that seems harmless at the moment simply because we know it would not be good in the long run.

But there are also decisions that are more challenge than decision. They are the good things that are placed before us, and our will to follow through is tested. When defeat seems sure, then is the time to begin to fight. Where others are quitting, then is the time to throw more strength into the battle. Anything worth having is worth working for, and is of lasting value.

Very often these sieges must be made silently and without seeming effort. And yet we know we cannot get something for nothing. We have a service to perform. We can make it a drudge, or we can make it a delightful experience, according to our faith.

Be persistent. Unless you do not particularly want your dreams to come true, you can't afford to know the meaning of apathy. You must continually be on the scene with the muscles of your mind toned.

It isn't difficult to have a dream. But it often ceases at that point. The willingness to follow through, the determination to look impossibilities in the eye and trudge on must be practiced before that dream can amount to anything.

All along life's road there are those who would discourage you, very often in ignorance, not realizing the effect of their words upon you. It is then that you must muster the strength to believe that theirs is only an opinion while your plans are based on the principle that all good things come to those who hustle while they wait.

It is too bad that they cannot see your invisible companions, persistence, faith, and a worthwhile plan. Smile and walk on.

There is a Divine Being with whom we can place all our

obstacles, all our doubts and fears—and then our work begins. We give lovingly of friendship, of any kind of help that we are capable of giving, of positive words and thoughts and understanding.

Give without thought of return. For while we are giving with loving selflessness, life shapes for us our heart's desire.

At night sometimes the world seems so topsy-turvy and you're so weary of doing things the same old way. Then nothing seems to please. . . . You try desperately for something new and different, something that doesn't seem so much like you. Why? Tonight you are different.

One cannot expect the world to be top side up all the time. Such perfection does not come so easily to the human nature. And always there is a search for something new and different. A change of pace . . . that thought that I don't want to be me today, to think my thoughts and do my daily chores. I want to make a complete change now, to know a whole new way of life. And it is good to leave behind the many daily situations that sometimes stand too closely to be seen clearly. But to be wise enough to know which things should be left behind.

There have been clean sweeps that have left behind the dearest things . . . and have taken along the same dreary, dark unhappy things of the mind that should have been left behind.

A line from the prayer of serenity is "The wisdom to know the difference. . . ." And wisdom, says Samuel Taylor Coleridge, is common sense in an uncommon degree. If one has the wisdom to wait a bit, wait until morning—or several mornings—that uncommon degree of common sense will give us the wisdom to know the difference.

We often wonder why we must come in contact with some phases of life that seem so unrelated to how we think and plan. It seems we should be able to proceed without stopping all along the way to contend with things that really have little kinship to what we're trying to do.

But no matter how we question and analyze, situations and events continue to present themselves for solving. It takes a great deal of wisdom to know the difference between that which we must do and that which we must refuse serious consideration. This very thin line is the deciding factor in the victory or defeat of any plan.

Like a well-written story, sometimes the smallest incident hidden among our experiences can play a very big part at some later time. It is difficult to know just which parts of the puzzle will fall into place to complete a picture we seek.

We must take one step at a time, being sensibly aware of the thoughts we store in our minds. For "as a man thinketh in his heart, so he is." As long as we dwell on all the unnecessary activities we will never have time for the important things. If we seek the wisdom of the one Creative Mind we have much less chance of being led astray by the glitter of unimportant things.

All of us have at sometime questioned our normalcy as human beings. We wonder why we did this or that, why we reacted to something so violently, or why we failed to react at all. An American author, Katherine Fullerton Gerould, has written, "The only glory most of us have to hope for is the glory of being normal." And for all our questionable actions sometimes, the normal person must be one who has felt not only the high points, but the low points of his emotions.

It is not the fact that someone has run the gamut of his emotions that makes him normal, but that he has had the ability to right himself before he could impose upon the rights of others.

The one that has never lost his temper, nor shed tears, nor refused to respond to other people, but stays day after day in light, shallow experience, has never known what it is to come into the center of the calm so richly appreciated.

All of us have made mistakes in behavior, some in ignorance, but more in bad taste. Perfection belongs to a Higher Source. It is ours to strive for, and our mistakes are to use in the growing-up process.

There comes a time when we have to turn a firm and deaf ear to those people who have no other intention than to disturb our peace of mind. There comes a time when we have to turn ourselves about in our very tracks and ignore the bitter complaining voice of experience.

There comes a time when we have to get angry with ourselves for allowing bad to become worse when there is someone bigger than we are who can handle everything.

There comes a time when we have to make a decision and to be so firm that it leaves no doubt in our minds that we know what we must do—and then do it.

There comes a time when we have to hear music and feel peace, or we have no foundation for living.

There comes a time when we must learn to appreciate and be thankful or lose all that matters to us.

There comes a time when we recognize the many faces of God as true blessings and give thanks.

Don't try to tell me what your enemy looks like. My enemy is lazy, a procrastinator that spends most of the time talking me out of success. My enemy says friends are fickle and true ones are most infrequent. Faith, I'm told, is not enough to carry me over barriers. And I'm not loved so much as others, but that's all right because what good is love?

The day is dreary, my enemy says, and the flowers at my feet will soon wilt. I shouldn't smile at anyone today because they won't smile back at me.

This will be one of those days when everything goes wrong, my enemy tells me, and if I do anything right someone else will get the credit. I should watch the clock and realize how long the day is and how weary I am.

Don't tell me about your enemy, I have one of my own. But the fact that I know my enemy makes all the difference. My enemy lies to me and wants to destroy me. So I'll refuse to give my enemy power this day by giving a special measure of love to my friends and know that everything is exactly opposite of what my enemy tells me.

Life offers us a great deal of stormy weather. In the beginning we are quite strong about it, taking things in our stride and moving confidently along. The things that test us seem to give us extra strength we didn't know belonged to us. And quite suddenly there is an awareness that enough is enough. But life doesn't know it, and the storm goes on and so do we.

Even though we are quite willing to give as long as we have to give, there seems to be no more stretch to the strength, either spiritually, mentally or physically. We question how much longer, how many more times we shall be able to reach into our bag of reserves to borrow another ounce of strength.

Of course, the first thing we must do is to take our minds off the thing as we do not want it, and begin to think steadily about how we do want it. It allows our creative minds to find the answers. It may mean we will have to wait awhile in the dark, but when the light comes, it is radiant.

There are many things that stay our feet along the way, but faith that this too will pass can make that way serene.

23

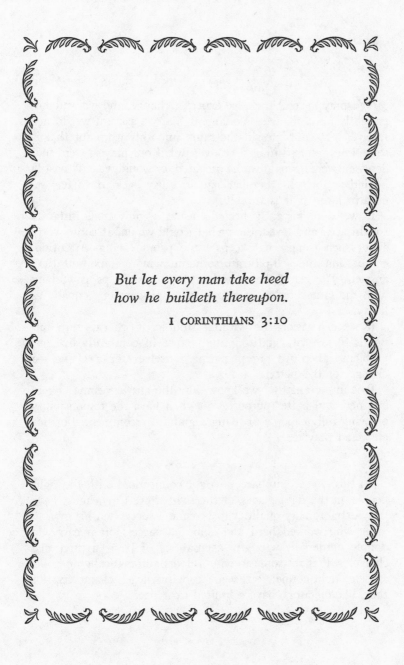

But let every man take heed
how he buildeth thereupon.

I CORINTHIANS 3:10

We pray for a change, we expect a change, and we wait impatiently for a change. We lament that we ask but we do not receive. Life continues in the same smoothly worn rut that is sometimes referred to as a groove. But if our prayers were suddenly answered, would we be prepared, or would we look hastily behind us for some familiar sign to hurry back to, to feel secure in, even if it is trouble.

If we were instantly healed, instantly prospered, instantly sought after and loved, then what would we do? It is the worry about such things that keeps some people going. Attention, compassion and self-pity are sometimes more important than answers. The fear of being without a purpose keeps us working with the same burden or allows us to pick up one equally as heavy.

If we can vision life without trouble, if we can turn our minds to joy with gratitude and refuse to constantly live our problems, then we are preparing ourselves for a change—a change for the better.

It is important that we know why the answers come. There is a new and better purpose. We then have the responsibility of being fully capable of living a grateful recommendation for answered prayer.

In this day of emphasis on right connections with the right people, in the right places, at the right time, a man must have truly extraordinary qualities to become a success on his own.

He who worked hard and achieved success often carries a double burden by wrongful accusations of being a privileged character. Perhaps some to whom doors automatically open because of right connections seem to be privileged characters, but they, like dictators, have a limited existence.

Having connections may help a man on the ladder of life, but it will never keep those rungs steady beneath his feet. Only his own greatness keeps him tall, sun-crowned. He must have something to give, something to offer before he can expect to be truly a privileged character. And then, he will have earned the right to his privileges. He is somewhat like God, blamed for much he didn't do and seldom given credit for the good he has done.

Whatever the future, the world still needs men like those J. G. Holland wrote about a half century ago: "God give us men. The times demand strong minds, great hearts, true faith, and willing hands. . . . Tall men, sun-crowned, who live above the fog, in public duty and in private thinking!"

How much voice do we really have in our own affairs? How free are we to speak out on the things we know and believe and want to say? How much voice do we have in public affairs?

How much goes unsaid because it may be bad for business, or it might make us look foolish? How often we should speak up but think it is none of our business. How quiet we are when someone's unethical hand does wrong.

What is it that inhibits man? His own fears. Fear of his own ignorance, fear of losing, fear of the bugaboos he knows lurk somewhere, but just isn't sure where.

Who is the man that is free of fears? The man who governs himself in such a manner and to have thought out his own ideas enough to be able to speak freely for himself.

Ethics would seem to be something to ignore if you wish to be successful in business. Many a person strives harder today than at any other time to divide his life so that being seen in church is good taste, and to be unethical in business to prove he is shrewd. Being successful isn't nearly as important as proving he got that way by the clever undoing of his opposition.

There was a time when building a better mouse trap by the most efficient methods gave man his satisfaction, but too often these days man is impressed because someone is smart. Not smart with intelligence, but smart with the cunning that goes along with the jungle code of getting before someone gets you.

The person who tries to get ahead by ethical methods, and by wanting only to provide something better than is in existence, must also be equipped to withstand having a little fun poked at him.

Frankly, the race of the tortoise and the hare is still on, and while the hare is tearing around showing off his ability to be a fast runner, the tortoise is making progress, and never losing his way.

Socrates being asked the way to honest fame, said, "Study to be what you wish to seem." Success takes time and moral discipline, but his success will be as a human being first, and then the crown of success in business will sit easily and firmly.

No prisoner ever loved his jail. And the same holds true for all kinds of prisoners, whether they be a dog on a leash or a human being tied to a responsibility. If they are there of their own free will and because they have a sense of belonging, the connecting link is made of love.

Responsible people with an assignment, and the feeling that it is theirs alone, will do it to the best of their ability and see it through. But if they must be watched and directed in every step, then it is a jail and the first thought is how to get out.

Freedom to be an individual with the right to make even small decisions is a precious possession. Freedom to come and go can build faith and trust within a person, to make him stick closer than a brother. The rigid rules and constant prodding of a free spirit will force him to find that freedom.

We simply cannot keep another in bondage without being in bondage ourselves. To hold humanity by invisible force is to keep constant watch. And even beneath that watchful eye there will be a continual search for escape.

Anyone completely dependent upon others must always bear their will-o'-the-wisp attitudes and the rising and lowering of the emotional tides. However, it is presumptuous of anyone to believe they could possibly be completely independent of others. Without other people, we could not exist.

But to believe we are doing our best for anyone except ourselves is to build on sand. Of course others inspire us. They give us reasons to be better. They give us the benefit of their experience, but we seldom learn from that. We demand experience of our own. So consequently, we err and make it right. We mar and erase. And sometimes we try and fail, but always it is up to us to decide whether we do better or worse.

We can despair easily if allowed to become completely and utterly dependent upon others. They are human and they make mistakes. But one must know some measure of forgiveness the same as he must know some independence, if only in the spirit. And if the spirit is free, then all else shall be too.

The setting of the sun on an old year is a kind of summing up time. What have you accomplished? What were your goals? Will they be higher in the new year?

Whatever the personal plans and whatever the reasons back of them, there is a common everyday sort of person that should be kept in view. He has a positive outlook, and you can best recognize him when he sincerely listens to a child's words.

You will see him when he steadies the elderly, you will know him by his kindness. You will not often hear his prayer as it is for his God. But you will know he is to be depended upon and that he will not tire of these things, for it is his natural role.

Think about this person when you set your plans. He is a good man to remember. Your success or failure depends upon this person being you.

A new galaxy of shining promises made to oneself are resolutions made with the utmost faith that self is listening and will carry out the plans.

But self is as unpredictable as a child playing in the street; it may dart in any direction, according to the mood and to whatever catches its attention. At the first sign of a challenge, self may race back and lean hard upon the old ways of doing things, no matter how wrong it may be. Resolutions do very little to change a way of living. They are easily made and easily forgotten. There may be a sincere desire to keep a resolution, but if self has not changed inwardly, little can depend on the outward change.

It is said that we promise according to our hopes and perform according to our selfishness. Failure to keep our promises to others is a disappointment, but failure within oneself is disaster.

A little performance is worth a host of promises on any day that starts a new year.

It is always amazing to hear someone scoff at the serious things. Perhaps they only scoff because they can't recognize anything really serious outside their own personal problems. . . . Or perhaps they are just afraid to acknowledge anything they don't understand.

Whatever it is that keeps people thinking in such a limited area adds to the residue of dullness in their minds. And until they can mature enough to believe in something worthwhile they continue to add layer after layer of residue to the mind.

It is not surprising that some people believe themselves in possession of all knowledge to the point that they feel free to ridicule those who are still in the process of thinking things out. We can never truly judge a man's reasoning. We can only see the results and with time it may be he will break through that accumulation to wisdom and kindness that is so necessary in tolerating others' opinions and beliefs. Then will the residue diminish and there will be a renewal of the spirit in mind.

Frequently quoted American editor and author Christian Nestell Bovee wrote that sensitiveness is closely allied to egotism—indeed excessive sensitiveness is only another name for morbid self-consciousness.

He wrote that the cure for it was to make more of our objects and less of ourselves. And it isn't easy to make less of ourselves.

Everyone at some time has felt extreme sensitivity toward people and surroundings. It is a sensitiveness that does not always have a good effect—seemingly for no reason at all we exercise no control over the emotions. It can be quite frightening to realize that we are quite as capable of destroying as we are, at other times, for building.

It is written in the essays of Aristotle that there are right things to say and a right way of saying them; and the same is true of listening. So often we make a casual remark, not meant to be tactless, but somehow it turns out that way. When there is a desire to appear witty, or clever, at someone else's expense, there should be no pride in the results.

And when we listen to someone's casual remark and take offense, we must examine our own thoughts. If we allow our minds to run in channels of vulgarity and mockery, then we can also expect to interpret others' words to mean the same things.

We can so easily read the wrong things into others' conversations, and in our own efforts to express ourselves say such foolish things that we lose the priceless gifts of relaxation and fun of conversing with other people. And for these reasons we must cultivate the art of speaking and listening with the warmest heart—which harbors nothing that is not right.

It is a good idea in the most sensitive times to recognize them for what they are and to make a pact within one's self to by pass this time for serious thought and decision making. This, above all, should be a time for relaxing against the wind of over-sensitiveness. To resist it only strengthens it, and to look at it clearly and coolly will take away its mystery and its heat.

It is well to remember that the too-sensitive person is not the true self, but the one with the marvelous mental attitude most certainly is—wait for him!

Remember all those times when you made three trips to the other room to get something, and before you got there you had already forgotten what it was? Didn't the thought of age dimming your memory enter your mind at those times?

There's really no need to waste time thinking that way. It is not the case of a scattered memory, but a skittery mind, jumping from one subject to another with only circumstances to remind you.

And haven't you awakened sharply in the middle of the night because suddenly you remembered something you should have done, or something you must do? Age again? No, it was the only time your subconscious mind ever found you quiet enough to remind you of something you wanted to remember.

Life would be so much more orderly if we took several minutes night and morning to sit completely away from outside sights and sounds to recall the important things. As long as we are able to see and hear the activity about us we have difficulty thinking soundly. The conscious mind is capable of carrying just so much, and then the debris must be cleared away before the "filed away" things in the subconscious can be remembered.

"Be still and know . . ."

It doesn't seem that a simple thing like going fishing could have such excellent results when the world suddenly seems too much. It is a very difficult thing to worry when your mind is fixed intently on a little red and white plastic float bobbing in the water.

Just taking one's mind off the general routine of living for even a short time is like a much needed and appreciated vacation. We seldom recognize the need for getting away from the monotony of following each day with another day exactly like it. We lose the value of the hours and minutes and lump them all together in things called days and plod along expecting miracles to come some day and save us.

The effort we have to give is in releasing the problem and concentrating on something beautifully simple and uncomplicated. Living doesn't seem so ominous when we can go fishing for a little peace and quiet and sidetrack the things that weigh so heavily on our minds.

Good health is such a blessing. And not everyone realizes how much he aids or harms his health. In fact, he gives much more thought to being careful not to get wet than being careful not to get angry. And it is said that anger can lower resistance to colds much quicker than getting wet.

It is a proven fact that to feel love builds a resistance to illnesses while resentment and hate can destroy both mind and body.

Longfellow once wrote that joy, temperance, and repose would slam the door on the doctor's nose. There's no doubt but that most doctors' noses are safe. But he, too, would be glad if more patients would exercise their ability to lift themselves out of much of their ill health by knowing some measure of joy rather than self pity, some healthy thoughts and less thought of self.

We lower our resistance to ill health in many ways, but none so surely works as worry, anxieties, and cares, plus our inability to recognize the fact that we are our own greatest enemy.

Surely there is nothing so peaceful to the eye as the quiet, soft-hued hills resting in the autumn sun. We think if we could only get to those hills we could walk in the warmth of that sunlight and feel that peace in every nerve and muscle.

But so frequently we are unable to follow our wills. We are forced to sit where we are. And the very thought of being bound to this spot sometimes makes us restless, perhaps beyond reason. Sometimes it creates a feeling of panic, that life will never be peaceful.

And then we look up into the limitless sky and see the depths and immensity of the universe, and we know that nothing binds us. That is, unless we want to be bound.

If we were to go to those hills, there would be others in the distance that would look as inviting. To hunt for peace outside ourselves is to ever be in search, and so to bind ourselves again.

33

But to loose that infinitely beautiful truth that peace is never there or there—but here, within me.

Most of us are lovers of familiar things. We love the routine of living, the security of knowing what is going to happen at a certain hour on a certain day. We love the knowledge that we will continue to love others even though we may not like what they are doing at the moment. We find great peace in knowing others will continue to love us even when we've been foolish.

The exciting and livable life is not always one of being on the go, being in entertaining places. The real life of life is not spangles that glitter and one continual round of gaiety.

Life is contentment, living in depth with a genuine love for work seasoned with recreation and freedom to worship where we choose and to pursue our talents as we please.

English author Samuel Johnson tells us that the fountain of content must spring up in the mind; and he who has so little knowledge of human nature as to see happiness by changing anything but his own disposition will waste his life in fruitless efforts.

Everyone develops his own way of centering his life on something. In his mind there is a design of what he thinks he is capable of being. If he wants to be what he thinks he is capable of being, then he must hold the design firmly in his mind until it is secured as the focal point.

Each life must have that focal point, that center of interest where all phases of life come together. A focal point gives strength and meaning to the smallest details of everyday living.

Dimension and depth belong to the life that is centered. Though it may take many forms we must always have a "home" to return to, knowing that here are the roots, the things that really matter.

There must be a blending of our lives with others. But to be happy with one's self, that focal point must be steady and true before we can feel contented that "all's right with the world."

34

There are two words in every life that mean more toward perfecting that life than any other thing. Those two words are the basis for every action. They are "personal responsibility."

Daniel Webster once wrote that the most important thought he ever had was that of his individual responsibility to God. It was his personal responsibility.

No matter how understanding others may be, how kind, and tolerant, there comes a time when we cannot ask, nor expect to receive, help in our struggle. There are simply times when other people cannot cover for our poor performance. It soon becomes time for us to stand on our own feet, express our own feelings, and search out our own beliefs.

Others can run interference for us, make excuses for us, and guess at our feelings. But we don't begin to live until we've accepted our personal responsibilities. We must learn to express truth in everything from showing our love to voting an election.

Life is one personal responsibility after another. Shifting it to another's shoulders loses some of the most important steps. Failure to recognize it is folly; ignoring it is stupidity, and accepting it is to find more truth and more strength than was ever imagined or expected.

At times, Americans seem too easily taken, too docile to political movements, and too indifferent to their own responsibilities as a free people. How easy it is to turn our heads and tell ourselves that there are intelligent people in high authority looking after our interests and that they will never let our freedom be lost. This kind of thinking is a fallacy. America still belongs to the people, and it is up to us to tell our representatives in Washington that we want it kept that way.

The Communists have a way of presenting themselves as true Americans and offering to the people a way that looks free and easy. These seemingly free handouts are securely fastened by invisible shackles to a carefully laid plan that will eventually take away our freedom unless we decide to personally do something about it.

Americans are known for their ability to start with a little ingenuity and a lot of faith to build powerful financial empires. But in great and small there beats a heart of devotion to God and country. In battle, no one could display more bravery, more determination or more loyalty than these defenders of America. In the face of seeming defeat, young Americans have stood together and fought courageously.

Now, people of all ages must stand together. We must make our views known to the government. We must continually develop within ourselves moral, physical, and spiritual strength; and we must pray to God—without that faith, all is lost.

Have you ever stood on the sidelines and watched the drama of your own difficulties being acted out in someone else's life? Does it provoke a feeling of gratitude that here I will witness something that will help me solve my own problem? Or does it invite a feeling of smugness that they were not so capable of hiding theirs as I have been of concealing mine.

Hiding one's difficulties can be compared to concealing an elephant. The only possible way to keep it a secret would be to keep it from those who could care less in the first place. If they were face to face with your elephant they would register little surprise and proceed immediately to forget it.

In fact, there is considerable danger in looking down on those who are trying to get their lives on the right track. At least they have the intestinal fortitude to try. And to pretend that one has nothing to overcome is merely polishing the front glass while the back door falls away.

Smugness or compassion? It was Cowper who reminded us, "Man may dismiss compassion from his heart, but God will never."

. . . *a man mine equal, my guide, and mine*
    acquaintance.
We took sweet counsel together, . . .

PSALMS 55:13, 14

Before we can share with others, we must have something to share. And all of us do have something to give. Not material things, but we can share our peace and our love and our loyalty.

Before we can share with others, there must be others with whom to share. For if we are selfish and self centered enough, we will never have to worry about sharing anything. We will be alone.

Before we can expect others to share with us, we must be capable of accepting. We must be worthy of others who desire to share with us; we must deserve their love.

Before the two of us can ever find anything in this world of mutual interest, we must have enough concern and enough love to feel a need within to produce something good enough to offer; not only to others, but to ourselves. If we have abused our own nature with thoughts of bitterness, harboring painful experiences, self condemnation for little progress regardless of circumstances, then we have nothing to offer.

The French philosopher Achille Poincelot once said, "Some people think that all the world should share their misfortunes, though they do not share in the sufferings of anyone else."

Two qualities so well liked in people are brightness and warmth, both parts of the sun. Sir David Brewster was a Scottish physicist of the eighteenth century. His study of the material world and its phenomena called the sun glorious, "the centre and soul of our system, the lamp that lights it, the fire that heats it, the magnet that guides and controls it, the fountain of color which gives its azure to the sky, its verdure to the fields, its rainbow-hues to the gay world of flowers, and the purple light of love to the marble cheek of youth and beauty."

What more beautiful qualities for any human being to pos-

38

sess than to have a soul at the center of its system, to light the appearance, to warm the feelings, to guide and control it through its colorful moods, and to let it rise as high as the azure skies and as wide as the gay world of flowers. But better yet, to be most beautiful with the purple light of love. What more to be given than the same qualities of the sun—by one Creator.

To live men need more than light, they need warmth. They need more than strength, they need grace. And more than all these they need love. There can be no greater joy than to see man's respect for man. The warmth and grace and love that bind together people in mutual concern.

Only when we can lay aside our personal feelings, our self concern and worry of our own gain, can we join in true communion and fellowship with others. And to feel a sense of belonging is necessary to man.

It is the nature, not only to be liked and wanted, but to like and want others. And in this relationship find not just warmth but light, not only grace but strength, and in all of these find love.

"Walk in the light and thou shalt see thy path, though thorny, bright; for God, by grace, shall dwell in thee, and God himself is light."—Barton.

Henry David Thoreau, whose love for simplicity often took him into solitude, also wrote of the sensitive side of man. "The finest qualities of our nature, like the bloom on fruits, can be preserved only by the most delicate handling."

How easy it is to destroy the only approach to man's true self. And how often communications are broken down by the brutal force of "getting to the point," and speaking "frankly."

The only time an agreement has been reached by the frankly route is when two people already believe in the same thing. And it is a most infrequent occasion when two people can meet head-on and believe the other honest because he is direct and wordy.

More often, there must be some thought given to the sensi-

39

tivity of the other person. First, he is a human being with human dignity. He has feelings and thoughts and he has strong likes and dislikes. And it is a considerate person who has the sensitive perception and insight into the heart of someone. And because of his thoughtfulness he can be more honest and direct and progress by it.

Nevertheless, if one has to be constantly on the outlook to keep from offending a friend, then he is not really a friend. It isn't difficult to be a friend to someone who endears himself to everyone. Indeed, it is a pleasure to be counted his friend. But it is another thing altogether to be a friend to someone who finds little friendship anywhere.

Other people seldom see us as we are. In fact, who we truly are is lost somewhere among our daily contacts. We react differently to nearly every person we meet. Their personality and ours may blend beautifully or it may clash horribly. And we can rather tell where the fault lies when we balance out the blends and the clashes. Are we easy to be friends with, or are we merely acquaintances and nothing more?

If people have to dodge around so many issues in order to keep us sweet, we need to hear some truth about ourselves. If we can't do it, it may have to come from a friend. Then, we must remember the words of Thomas à Becket, "Better are the blows of a friend than the false kisses of an enemy."

Have you considered the effect your presence may have on people around you? Do they need you? The answer is yes. We are somewhat selfish with our presence at times. We want to withdraw and think our own thoughts and read quietly rather than entertaining someone or just listening to them. But we never really know how much they need us, not to perform good deeds for their good, but only to be company to share a happening of the day.

Perhaps within their minds we can quiet some restlessness, assure them that they are needed, or give them a feeling of tranquillity. To many life is no simple matter, and to hear them out may be the remedy.

It has been said by a very wise man that if you never make a mistake you're not doing anything.

It is a relief to know that every day, without fail, we come in contact with people who put such confidence in us that we strive ever harder to never fail. Such people build human beings —and there is no job more worthy, or more creative.

Building character and confidence in a human being is a delicate task . . . for no two people respond in the same way. A challenge may be the way to boost one up, while another may need encouragement and praise to guide him on the way. But, oh, how human we all are, having the need for accomplishment . . . for attention . . . for approval.

And how great the responsibility for leaders who must have the wisdom to inspire . . . the integrity to trust . . . the heart to understand. The race is hard for leader and follower, for each must understand the other—and there must be compassion for the slow, courage for the weak, and appreciation for the loyal. To follow one must be secure; to lead one must be very wise.

It should be the practice of all of us that when we hear something complimentary about someone to tell them. It is so true that man does not live by bread alone, and to be recognized in having done something that rated approval is a very great reward.

Nothing so builds character in a child than to let him know someone believes he has a fine potential. That feeling that "someone believes in me" can be the very thing that will anchor his faith deep in hope for humanity.

To be able to see the good acts of others renders a service to ourselves. Swiss theologian John Casper Lavater once said, "He is incapable of a truly good action who finds not a pleasure in contemplating the good actions of others."

Appreciation for the achievement of others is akin to sunshine—we simply can't help it shine on other people without feeling the glow ourselves.

Every year at the time of festive paper, gay ribbons and shimmering tinsel, we hear at least once, "Christmas has become so commercialized." Christmas is whatever we make it. If we contribute to the commercializing of Christmas by choosing gifts begrudgingly, giving thought only to the dollar spent but never to the spirit of giving, then by our own minds we are losing sight of the most beautiful time.

In the face of those who miss the true meaning of Christmas are the happy people whose lives are based on the gift they share. There's a simplicity in their shopping, but there is splendor and great joy in the gift of light they shed.

Their presence is a silent blessing, their words are cheerful, and they smile with kindness. These truly beautiful gifts of sincerity give a rise to the heart that cannot be matched. They are basically the one gift that God gave us called Christ—the priceless gift of love.

If at Christmastime you receive one gift called love, you have received the best gift of all. The genuine product is never packaged, never purchased and impossible to commercialize. And the most delightful and heartwarming time to receive it is right after having given it.

It is said that it is not the amount of food, but the cheerfulness of the guests that make the feast. And when we consider that we are guests at the table of life, we must also decide whether we are making it a feast or a famine.

In fact, we are living evidences of whether our lives are feasts or famine. Everything we feed ourselves, whether it be thought, word, deed or bread is written upon our physical and spiritual lives.

To think of feasting brings to mind a table laden with different and delicious dishes. But, deep in our thoughts we know a feast is only a meal without the light and warmth of others. The cheerfulness would be replaced by a meager existence. There would be no laughing faces, no sensing that all is well because love dwells at that table.

42

And so to share our lives in that manner is to make living a feast. But to withhold our friendship, to know no close communion and happiness is to feel the barrenness of famine.

❧Cooperation is said to be the essence of success. Without it confusion and chaos are the ruling factors and inharmony the main thought. Cooperation is a result of excellent leadership, the ability to build a team of loyal players who can follow instructions or think for themselves, whichever is for the best of all concerned.

A team is a group with specific parts to play. In all wisdom they know a little about every part, but they play their own position with precision and efficiency.

Every player cannot be captain, and every person cannot play quarterback. The part may be small, but if it is played with fairness and dignity and to the utmost of ability, then it will be as important to the successful outcome or result as the biggest job in the organization.

The practical view of cooperation is vivid in John Dickinson's words, "By uniting we stand; by dividing we fall." We are only as strong as the weakest, only as cooperative as the spirit in which we work.

❧In this jet age when almost "instant there" is commonly accepted, the world has become very small. The days of clinging to one's own birthplace is most infrequent, and those who never dreamed of traveling have adjusted themselves to it quite well.

And with shorter distances between man and his neighbor it seems their worlds should find more opportunities for mutual understanding. But we must realize that even though our material worlds may be easily crossed, our thoughts are worlds apart. Until we can bring together a thinking people with the desire to create living conditions that are peaceful and full of kindness, fast travel can waver between good and bad.

A British novelist and poet, George Moore, said, "It is thought, and thought only, that divides right from wrong; it is thought, and thought only, that elevates or degrades human deeds and desires.

The greatest tragedy of life is not that we quarrel with our fellowman, but that we do not take time to know him.

In his great understanding of man and nature, Thoreau wrote, "Let a man take time enough for the most trivial deed. . . ." Take time.

How often what seems to be an unfriendly atmosphere is only a lack of time. Some of our dearest friends are hidden behind the mask of hurry. And we need so desperately to know each other.

Understanding comes when people are allowed to talk to one another. They discover the ways and needs, the loves and hopes, and the despairs and fears when they take enough time to speak of them. All these things that make for understanding and compassion come from personal contact and the knowledge and practice of good will.

People become more civilized, more peaceful, more as God intended them to be when they take time to make friends out of acquaintances.

To be a good listener endears many a friendship. Everyone needs someone with whom to talk at length on all subjects without later regret. It has been written, "What a great blessing is a friend with breast so trusty that thou mayest bury all your secrets in it."

And how often we need to be that friend and be the listener, and to make sure we are worthy of that trust.

Listening comes in many ways. We listen with all our senses, knowing many times without having to be told what someone's needs are. Charles Dickens said that no one is useless in this world who lightens the burden of it for anyone else. And it just may be by listening that we lighten another's load.

Sometimes we listen with our hearts and understand in silence. Sometimes we simply have to put ourselves into a situation to understand all sides of it. And we best do so by listening.

All our lives we carry secrets with us that we long to reveal to someone who understands.

There are relationships in our lives better and closer than the ordinary. Closer yet than brothers are those with whom we can share all our secrets, we think.

What a sad state of affairs when life imparts that man cannot always be trusted. What a shock to realize we have given all our hearts and bared our souls to someone whose curiosity was the only motive that compelled him to listen.

Phillip Massinger, sixteenth-century poet, once wrote, "I have played the fool, the gross fool to believe the bosom of a friend would hold a secret mine own could not contain."

Not one living soul can testify that he has nothing within his life and thoughts that he cannot reveal. And many have not expressed their innermost thoughts because they have found no one in whom they can confide.

As Shakespeare said, "Many a man's tongue shakes out its master's undoing." Sometimes the loquacious tells his secrets, not because he wants to tell them but because he loves to talk.

One of the greatest feelings in the world is to discover we haven't told something we cherish very much to someone we once thought we could trust.

A graphologist is a handwriting analysis expert who can take apart the loops and dashes of anyone's penmanship and tell him about his nature. We have a natural curiosity about ourselves. We want to know whether our self-image is the true one. We often think we are capable of seeing another's true nature, but we seem to lack the ability to really know ourselves. In fact, so much about us reveals our disposition and temperament that it can be distressing.

Our handwriting may tell us about our emotional natures, and we may learn that we are introverts by the slant of our letters, but much of our disposition can be self-analyzed by the way other people respond to us.

It doesn't take a graphologist to tell us that if we are inconsistent in our friendliness, if the tongue alternates acid and honey, if we continually complain, continually gossip, criticize and pout, we are revealing a nature we too often think is hidden.

Each time I hear the ringing bells and Auld Lang Syne, I sigh
Another year has slipped away and I haven't told you why
You've meant so very much to me in moments that we've shared.
You gave me courage to go on when I thought nobody cared
I've seen you smile when tears were near,
I've felt your courage where there could be fear.
I've heard your honesty when the false pressed hard,
And your joys and loves hate could not retard.
There must be times when there are concealed
Feelings and thoughts you have not revealed.
But in the New Year I promise to be
More thoughtful of you and less conscious of me
Time knows no other but to slip gently away,
But Happy New Year, my child, shall be yours every day!

No one seems to be interested in our excuses—they merely want performance. Alibis for lack of service, for lack of ability to give a full measure of trust makes a bad servant. And we are all servants, serving each other in one way or another.

It is an unhappy one that someone does not depend upon for something. There is great satisfaction in being needed, even to the point of doing more than one is capable of doing.

English divine Sidney Smith once wrote, "Try to make at least one person happy every day, and then in ten years you may have made three thousand, six hundred and fifty persons happy, or brightened a small town by your contribution to the fund of general enjoyment."

We cannot move a step upon this earth without finding someone to serve. And as we serve each day, we never stop to consider how many we've made happy; but it should be very vivid in our minds how many we've made unhappy.

As long as there has been a human race there has been someone crying out, "No one understands!" Somewhere along the way communications have broken down and the result is misunderstanding.

To be misunderstood is painful. We keep wanting to explain and explain until we get our message across. Sometimes it is the lack of the wise use of words. Then, it may be an unwilling ear. But whatever the race, the politics, sophisticated or home grown, everyone has the desire to be understood. They want every motive, every mood, completely and unquestionably understood.

But to be completely understood can also have its rebound. A goddess can turn into a woman, and a hero can slip into a man when only one of their moods is completely understood.

Understanding breeds familiarity. Familiarity may not breed contempt, but it can certainly take the edge off the mystery. And, it is mystery that keeps life interesting.

In all wisdom, man should worry much less about having himself completely understood, and make a more diligent effort to understand others.

Something dies within us when no one cares. It is a circumstance of our own making when we have failed to give to another the thought and concern that would have helped when it was most needed.

Sorrows can be borne because others care. Greatness can be achieved because someone cared. To care is our purpose.

Who knows but that these small acts of sympathy and understanding may place another life into the one slot on the jig-saw puzzle of life.

If we were all the things we expect of others, the result would be perfection. We would be perfect in forgiveness, faithful in love, and devoted to the welfare of others. Such excellence has never been accomplished, except that we work continually for it. To work for it, we have to care. And for someone to care is the thing that matters.

"Instead of allowing yourself to be so unhappy, just let your love grow as God wants it to grow; seek goodness in others, love more persons more; love them more impersonally, more unselfishly, without thought of return. The return, never fear, will take care of itself."—Henry Drummond.

If you've ever been alone in a strange place, you're bound to know how wonderful it is to have someone make you feel welcome.

Many people have the knack for being at home in whatever place they find themselves. And in this gift they find no loneliness to tug at them, but more often than not most of us feel like strangers. And in doing so set ourselves apart, or make it sometimes questionable as to the wisdom of asking us into a friendly circle.

A friendly face and a friendly voice can make the most timid soul feel welcome. It can make them feel at home. For in the midst of many there is loneliness. Perhaps it is because our feigned look of self sufficiency made someone question our need for help.

Many a door has opened, and many a sound friendship won when someone said, "We're glad to have you . . ." The very atmosphere can be charged with concern when we see someone who cannot find his way. The warmth of divine love is for daily use in making someone feel welcome.

We should not forget nor fail to see the wisdom of Hebrews 13:2: "Be not forgetful to entertain strangers: for thereby some have entertained angels unaware."

There must be no stronger feeling in the hearts of most people than the desire to belong. To belong to something, to someone, and in a place where the feeling is warm and friendly. The most blessed child in town is the one born and raised in the same neighborhood and has the tightly knit sense of belonging to everyone. Suddenly the child is not just a child of his parents, but a child of everyone in the church, in school and anywhere where there is warmth and love and peace.

War rages within so many, disallowing them any connection or any strand of love that would tie them to anything that gives them a sense of security. And when people become insecure they become demanding. And in demanding they lose the most essential part—the ability to attract love to them simply by loving first.

In the words of William Blake: "Love seeketh not itself to please. . . . Nor for itself hath any care. . . . But for another gives its ease. . . . And builds a Heaven in Hell's despair."

Some of my most productive moments are not when I consider how evil the world is, but how powerful is my God.

Some of the best times are not all when I'm enjoying life, but when those I love are knowing happiness.

The highest peak of wealth comes when the joy within surpasses anything I can create out here.

The bloom of good health is felt more richly when I let it flow through me rather than dwelling on the possibility of sickness.

Friendships are strongest and most true when I don't worry about giving more than I receive.

In order that others forgive me, I must also learn to forgive.

I must never forget that negative thoughts feed on fear and starve on faith.

One of the greatest mistakes I can make is to believe myself to be without friend or faith or opportunity.

These personal proverbs belong to every thinking person who wants his life to have more meaning, know more happiness and feel more richly the love that is the medicine for the sickness of the world.

49

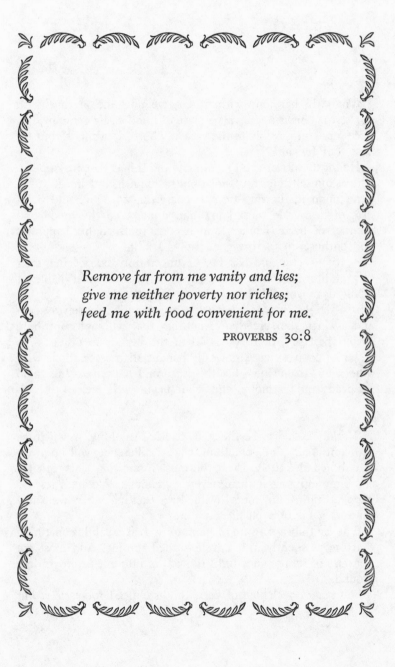

Remove far from me vanity and lies;
give me neither poverty nor riches;
feed me with food convenient for me.

PROVERBS 30:8

To be in harmony with others, we must be in tune with ourselves. This is not always a state of mind easily come by, but necessary and possible to the person who truly wants to put his best foot forward.

He must cultivate and recultivate the things that make peace within himself. He must not only have faith, but he must depend upon it, drawing from it energizing joy, love and lightness of heart. He must know and understand the mood and manner of his co-workers and express to them his happiness and enthusiasm for the good things of life.

At times everyone has fits of uncertainty concerning their way of life. And it is gratifying to have someone capable of lifting us out of the blues and scattering the doldrums. But the job is mainly ours. We have to cross examine ourselves again and again to be sure there's nothing that will not contribute to our best self, or draw less than the best from others.

To be cooperative is not only beneficial to associations with others, but to our own health, peace and happiness. Let there be peace and harmony, and let it begin with me.

Variety is said to be the spice of life. Anything in which we can continually find something new, a difference, will hold our attention indefinitely. Even the most interesting work can become monotonous if there never is a change. We are a restless people, finding life more livable and exciting when we know there is a bit of a change in store.

One isn't always aware of monotony. It is a subtle something that creeps silently into a well formed routine. And most are unaware of its presence until its victim, interest, begins to lose ground.

Sometimes a change of pace fulfills a need for variety, but

the most satisfying is one's ability to lay aside a regular routine to lend a hand to a neighbor when he needs it.

The very old and happy habit of helping one's neighbor never found a man bored. His heart was light, not because he searched for variety, but because it found him when self was forgotten and the need to help a neighbor was the only thought.

There seem to be two important things to do in time of difficulty. One is to pray and the other to keep one's sense of humor. The first is essential to make the basic correction and the other is necessary to balance the human spirit while things work out.

Without a sense of humor, one tends to become too serious about the personal self. It becomes all too important, too self-righteous and far too self-centered.

At the first signs of trouble, a person wants to find some one wiser in whom to confide and ask questions. And their advice may be most helpful, but it is still the responsibility of the human being to get himself off his back and do it with dignity and self-respect that will not lower his standards nor cause him embarrassment. And humor can help him do it.

There is humor in every situation if we can detach ourselves from the seriousness of it long enough to look for it. Abraham Lincoln knew the importance of his sense of humor and said, "With the fearful strain that is on me night and day, if I did not laugh I should die."

If we could but read it, every human being carries the marks of his character in the lines of his face. The very expression is etched there by habitual thought. The most beautiful features may be blank of expression, lacking depth of thought or understanding, while the plainest face may be lighted with a radiance only sincerity and inner beauty can produce.

Alexander Smith was a Scottish poet who wrote, "On your

53

features the fine chisels of thought and emotion are eternally at work."

No pretense can hide the thoughts and feelings. The narrowed eyes of suspicion and discontent tattle, while serenity and devotion to others can reveal such beauty of spirit that the shape of the face is forgotten.

"In thy face I see the map of honor, truth, and loyalty" wrote Shakespeare, and it is safe to say that being able to see those things in another's face is an assurance that he also had such a face. To see only avarice and selfishness in every expression turned to us is to know that our own expressions lack something to be desired.

Life does not have to be full of ease to reflect beauty. Some of the most beautiful faces in history have not had eyes to see nor voices to move their lips, but have possessed peace and serenity that only faith could render.

All the world listens for the voice that speaks with its heart.

How important is the tone of voice, no matter what position we hold in life. The voice of authority, the demanding, commanding and authoritative voice has little lasting effect upon its audience. But the voice of kindness, the cheerful and friendly voice creates receptivity that few can resist.

In the words of Longfellow, "How wonderful is the human voice! It is indeed the organ of the soul. The intellect of man sits enthroned, visibly, on his forehead and in his eye, and the heart of man is written on his countenance, but the soul reveals itself in the voice only."

The voice on the telephone creates a picture for the listener. With the business of the world being run to a very great extent by telephone, it is of the utmost importance what sort of picture that should be. No matter how sharp, strong, hard, flat, weak or soft, that voice creates an impression. If only we could have our voices recorded and hear them played back, what a shock it would be to so many to hear themselves in exactly one of those categories.

Even animals and children respond to voices as they truly are. All the actions in the world speak loudly, but the voice of love, the voice of friendship, and the voice of encouragement is the sweetest of all sounds.

The truly sincere quality in the voice is from the nature within, springing from concern for those about us, the divine love, the deep feeling for all of life.

America's art critic Henry Theodore Tuckerman believed the hand to be the mind's own perfect subject. As physical labor shows in a man's hands, so does illness, or greediness, or strength.

No other part of the body so expresses human behavior. With our hands we work, play, communicate, love, and express our fear, joy and grief. These beautifully sensitive symbols of faith, love and friendship are the hands of time that never stand still. They clasp to us the things we love, the books we read, the seeds we plant, the stitches we sew, and the civilization we build.

This marvelously made human hand, directed by the mind's eye, the mind's ear, and the heart's desires, works every waking moment to express its owner's life.

The gentle touch, so closely linked with our emotions, can also be the unmistakable expression of strength and honesty. And the most beautiful of all, the praying hands, for surely they are conscious only of God.

A lady of much wisdom has often remarked, "If you want to feel well all the time and feel alive, you have to keep the rhythm in your body." Rhythm, the gentle, easy flow of life.

Ordinarily we think of keeping time with music when we think of rhythm. The very idea of allowing one's self the frivolity of feeling rhythm—and such a wonderful idea!

There is an underlying rhythm to all of living. Wherever there is life, there is that pulsating rhythm that has everything on the move. There is harmony and there is a subtle smoothness to finding one's own pace. When we get out of step and resist that pace, we have "one of those days" when everything goes wrong.

William Shakespeare wrote, "The man that hath no music in himself, nor is not moved with concord of sweet sounds, Is fit for treasons, stratagems, and spoils; the motions of his spirit are dull as night, and his affections dark as Erebus. Let no such man be trusted."

Leisure—what is it? It is that beautiful something that escapes us most of the time. Leisure, like most everything else, can be found if we truly want it. We seem to have the ability to do most of what we set our minds to do, and the less important things can be set aside for this particular thing.

We get pretty stale when we never take time to relax. After a few hours of getting away from even a beloved madhouse will make a new human being out of a bundle of nerves.

Pursuit of leisure is to lose it. We can't suddenly say that the next five minutes will be for complete relaxation. It takes that long to begin to unwind. Gaiety and rhythm and frivolity are shunned by most minds. But if there are none of these, even in the smallest amounts, then leisure is more of a restless shuffling —like a night out with no place to go.

We need to exercise our minds a little to achieve any goal, and leisure is definitely a goal!

Did you know that when a person pokes fun at someone else he's covering up his own embarrassment?

Everyone has shortcomings, peculiarities about themselves they have no pride in nor want others to know about. So, frequently they call attention to the "different" traits of others. Sometimes we believe they are not aware of their own problems, but they are. They are superconscious of them, and because of it they must escape through finding something about someone else they believe is worse than their own.

The truly wise person is one who takes his own unique qualities and builds around them. Some of the most fascinating people are those who surround their unusual features with such exquisite mannerisms and beautifully developed personalities so handsomely as to make others ordinary.

It has been written by Augustine, "This is the very perfection of a man, to find out his own imperfection."

There's a song that says ". . . it ain't necessarily so," and it certainly isn't! How often we accept someone's casual remarks as fact. Even appearances can be misleading. But, knowing this, we still have a tendency to take a thread and build a yard of cloth.

It makes all the difference in the world what we believe. To simply accept an opinion, even our own when hastily formed, indicates a lack of sound thought.

We sometimes have the failing of believing everything we hear. But it is far wiser to know, with certainty, the facts about a teaching by looking at its followers.

The eyes and ears of our hearts and spirits are often more accurate in determining right from wrong than we can expect from normal hearing and seeing. However blessed we are to have our faculties, we are still in dire need of that sixth sense known as common sense.

Only the very foolish can close their eyes to truth and accept without question the many issues of life that face us daily. Surely men must form opinions and carry on, but we need those who have the ability to think clearly and truthfully. All else is merely opinion.

All things in sequence, first the bud and then the flower. We can no more hold back the blossom than we can the daylight. It is inevitably there, beautifully delicate and subject to crushing. Only through very careful tending will it withstand the winds and rain and pressures of the outside.

Sequence is the order of human life. God intended us to unfold as the flower. First the seed in fertile soil, the birth, the growth, the learning, the discoveries, the knowledge, the desires, the fulfillment as each phase of life follows its own sequence. We hold back the flowering of life only if we want it to be nonexistent. For it must progress, and in some of the most tender spots progression must be slow, easy, and reverently handled, for it can be as fragile as the flower.

Especially in woman is the delicacy of thought which entwines itself throughout her being, crossing from phase to phase, creating within her conflicts not easily understood. Something out of sequence in one phase may postpone the flowering of another phase. The very roots of her soul must be watered with reverence to successfully follow the sequence of life. If no other human understands or cares to understand, if she does, then continues—first the bud and then the flower.

Of all the intricate and complicated creations in the world, man occupies the first place. His life is made up of such flexuous combinations of body, soul, and spirit that he does not even understand himself.

It is every thinking man's desire to know what makes him tick and how to go about making himself tick better. Whether he realizes it or not, man is in search of the truth of his own being. Why is he here? What step should he take next? One problem after another, question after question brings him to this place again and again.

It is his personal problem and the wisest of persons cannot give him the answers. He will always need help to encourage him in his search, but he must go within himself to cure, to live, to feel, to believe.

Man must win his own heart before he can find happiness with others. He must know what he wants and be willing to share it with others for it is written that life is made up, not of great sacrifices or duties, but of little things, in which smiles, and kindnesses win and preserve the heart.

English divine John Mason wrote these words, "By these things examine thyself: By whose rules am I acting; in whose name; in whose strength; in whose glory? What faith, humility, self-denial and love of God and to man have there been in all my actions?"

Are you one of those people who degrade themselves in idle conversation until it becomes a fact within your mind? Has it become your belief that this is true humility, that by taking down your abilities, hiding your light, refusing to accept your rights as a child of God as being meek and humble?

This thing called life is given to us for a purpose, never to downgrade; no more than we should blow it out of proportion by thinking too highly of ourselves.

Each life is important, each breath for a purpose, each moment a time for learning. Walt Whitman has written in "Leaves of Grass": "Whoever you are! motion and reflection are especially for you; the divine ship sails the divine sea for you. Whoever you are! you are he or she for whom the earth is solid and liquid, you are he or she for whom the sun and moon hang in the sky, for none more than you are the present and the past. For none more than you is immortality."

By our words we reveal our minds. It is so easy to refuse to be a channel through which the best can reveal itself. And it is so easy to forget that our song of life, as Whitman has written, "The song is to the singer, and comes back most to him. I swear the earth shall surely be complete to him or her who shall be complete!"

The human being worries a great deal about what others think. It is a nagging worry that somehow the curtain that protects his privacy from the eyes of the world will suddenly drop and allow them to see all the things his pride has hidden.

Why is it that we seemingly need to be clever in order to "handle" the world. Why can't we just live honestly and openly, without scheming and trying to appear that we are something we are not. The world is so heavy laden with priggish pride that the clean, simple truth is lost in playing it "cool." Why can't we quit being something pent up inside and be something like sunshine or showers right out here where we can enjoy it or get over it.

Socrates said that the shortest and surest way to live with honor in the world is to be in reality what we would appear to be. And we may just as well, because if there isn't a good cake under all that frosting, someone is going to know it anyway. To drop all the pretense and say with genuine honesty, "This is the way I am" would be to find a whole new way of enjoying the simplicity of being oneself.

Is there ever a perfect time? A wise mother says there isn't. She advises us to take life by the hand and march right into the middle, and then start digging out the corners. She says not to wait for a perfect time to do anything, because a perfect time never quite makes it. We simply have to go ahead and make it as near perfect as possible.

A perfectionist is usually someone who can never find the perfect way, and gives up in futility. But the one who aims at perfection and does not wait for it, is at least moving and there's nothing useless about that. Unless one is moving, he resembles Tennyson's description: "Faultily faultless, icily regular, splendidly null, dead perfection; no more."

We have to face life, not under the pressure of perfection, but by pure faith. We have to go on accepting and rejecting as we come to each phase.

"For perfection does not exist," said eighteenth-century writer Alfred de Musset. "To understand it is the triumph of human intelligence; to expect to possess it is the most dangerous kind of madness."

In the rush of too much to do, we stack up for ourselves things we are going to do, things we ought to do, and things we intend to do. We do first the things of necessity, we take time to think a little about what we ought to do, and the rest is left to good intentions.

Frequently the good intentions hold the key to our happiness. While we bog down in the necessities of living, the things that mean so much slip away unnoticed.

We always expect other people to know that we intended to do this or that, but we must realize that they cannot read our good intentions. Good intentions have the same look as nothing at all. And people have to draw their own conclusions as to what our thoughts and feelings are. Only if we express them can we ever hope for others to know what we would like to do, even though circumstances may hinder us.

It has been written that an intelligent being has what it takes to surpass himself. By sensible thought we can actively express our good intentions and this opens the way for fulfillment.

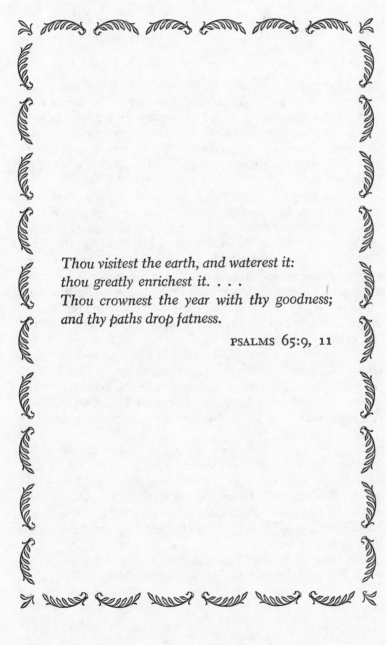

Thou visitest the earth, and waterest it:
thou greatly enrichest it. . . .
Thou crownest the year with thy goodness;
and thy paths drop fatness.

PSALMS 65:9, 11

Realizing that there is a multitude of wonderful things to appreciate, we must shake them all together in our minds and wait for the chosen ones to rise to the top like bubbles. Life is such a challenge, such a joy to live when it is appreciated. If we could only realize who gave us life, we would understand even more why He intended us to appreciate and love all that is about us.

The things we can appreciate are never in any particular order, but mingled together as they are in our lives. We can so beautifully and joyfully appreciate the sound of our children's laughter when sudden happiness overtakes them; the tremendous and moving power of silent prayer; a strong voice singing a song of inspiration, or of sentiment; early morning sunrises, misty pink and fresh; a mockingbird singing out his heart in the depth of night; the touch of souls in understanding; violin music; and our children in prayer, in spells of delight, or in any other moment.

To name them all would be an impossibility, to live them all is a blessing. We must not pass these things by without appreciating them. We must not lose them by failing to give thanks. These are the things we always have near us, and we can appreciate them merely by attuning our senses to them.

Henry David Thoreau, whose cry was "Simplify! Simplify!," went to great measures to prove to himself, and perhaps to society, that life could be lived in the most simple manner and at the least expense. With only a few dollars he managed to provide for himself the things of absolute necessity for quite a long period of time.

Not many of us would care to exist on the absolute necessities. We have become too much accustomed to easier living.

Things that were once thought of as luxuries are now considered necessities. And yet, with all of this, life is anything but simple. We seem to have the ability to complicate the best laid plans and find ourselves shadow boxing.

Like many of the trite old adages, "life is what we make it" is so true. By our own minds we accept or reject, by ignoring or by searching out the causes of shadows and removing the cause. It is whatever we elect to do about our individual lives that makes the difference. But we shall make great strides when we recognize the supreme excellence in all things of simplicity.

One needn't ever be worried about doing without the necessary things in life—if he has a grateful heart. A grateful heart is not just remembering to write a few words to someone who has done a kindness, or saying thank you graciously and at the right moment. A grateful heart is the feeling of great blessing which precedes that thank you note and that verbal expression.

A grateful heart is one that always knows the fullness of that rich feeling of first being grateful without cause. And then, all other gratitude and its expression comes naturally.

Perhaps true gratitude is a grateful thought toward heaven that I should be chosen to fill this spot, do this work, and have been given the strength to do it.

It was Romaine, the English theologian, who said, "Gratitude to God makes even a temporal blessing a taste of heaven." We can have so much more heaven with a grateful heart.

Today I heard the laughter of children at play. Their voices filled the air almost like chimes. And I felt their arms about my neck and their sticky kisses on my face. How lucky I am! Today I heard a mockingbird trilling out every single song he ever heard from his winged friends. I closed my eyes and in the trees I heard all the voices I've heard since childhood, and it took me through all the happy, breathless, precious times I loved so much.

Today I heard my mother's voice calling to me happily. It was a good, strong, healthy voice that has called to me courage, and hope and peace, and shall continue to call down many lanes to me.

Today I heard my child's voice. I heard her singing, I heard her praying, I heard her laughing and talking. I heard her teasing and moving from place to place in all the activities I love to see her in.

Now, even more than ever I realize how grateful I am that God has given me the excellent faculty of hearing. I shall with all diligence try to hear nothing evil, but only love and peace which is my heritage.

I don't know of anyone I'd rather find happiness than you. Perhaps somewhere along the way you'll also find what causes it and maybe it will be something you can find within your heart to share with others . . . for only in sharing are we ever really happy.

Just remember that it may well be where you least expect it. You may recognize it as something you're about to give away. . . . But don't worry, it will come back so many times; like love, it seeketh not its own but flies over us like angels. And when it finds a heart big enough to hold all the love it can supply it settles itself, wings and all, within the soul of that love.

And then the world will be new. There will be sights you've never seen and they've been there all the time . . . music you've listened to, but never heard before . . . there will be laughter from the heart . . . and gratitude for all of life's privileges. There will be peace and contentment . . . and strength abounding to withstand all adversity . . . and quiet acknowledgment of God. For without Him, there could be none of these.

Have you ever known someone whose very presence comforted you? They seem to have no need of words, but their quiet companionship soothes like balm to the soul. These are your kindred souls who have already been the route you're traveling, or are just ahead and leaning back to take your hand.

Wherever you are on the path of life, there have been many there before you. It may seem the loneliness of the road has many empty echoes. But there have been many good people concerned enough to make an effort to mark the rougher places to allow your journey easier traveling.

And like all travelers we must look for those signs and to make them more plain to the ones who will follow.

And then, in quiet communication, we can each take our turn by understanding.

How often we see someone who desperately needs our help. We would like to help him, but we put it out of our minds because it seems beyond our means and beyond our strength. We use the excuse that we have enough problems of our own without going out on a limb for someone else. Charity begins at home and at home and at home.

If we have the true desire, and the welfare of someone else in our sights, we can ask divine guidance, and we will receive help. If help does not come, it is because we were not truly serious. Or perhaps whatever we wanted to do was not in the best interests for all concerned. Our help may have slowed his progress or weakened his efforts. If our desires are worthy we need have no fear that a way will come to help.

The desire to help is a divine gift, and we accept it most beautifully by using it.

No hope? How foolish, for as long as there is a breath of life there is hope. How many people have sprung to their spiritual feet at the challenge of "no hope" and proved there is always hope. Perhaps there's nothing you can do for me, or I for you, but then again, perhaps there is.

As long as I do not impose the thought of hopelessness on you, and you do not convince me that your strength is all I can depend upon, then there is hope.

The things we sometimes call "miracles" are merely hopes activated by faith. And a wise teacher has said, "Give thanks for that which you need and soon you will have that for which you have given thanks."

If hope seems to elude you, let us give thanks that it is ours again. Let us speak words that are positive and reassuring and throw ourselves unreservedly into faith and trust, disregarding every emotion that seeks to convince us otherwise.

To lie down and be discouraged is our temptation, but to hope and have faith is our wisdom.

There are so many things we must come to know. If there are obstacles we have made them. And if there is unrest it is because of a lack of holiness, of recognizing the truly important. If our appetites are too great, it is not that we crave food or drink, but something higher than that which we are experiencing.

Sometimes we fail to know the needs of others, but more often we can see their needs more clearly than we can our own. And we can help ourselves quickly by recognizing the truth of our own being.

We are spiritual beings and to operate in the strict physical and mental sense is likened to running a car with only gasoline. It cannot be done efficiently. It takes water, gasoline, and oil.

When we learn that it takes our physical, mental and spiritual beings to make one person, then we are whole and have eliminated the inability to help ourselves. The outcome depends on you and me. And it is our duty to disqualify the thousand and one excuses that keep us from that duty.

Most successful ventures have behind them some hardships. We, as human beings, demand such experiences before we can truly appreciate the meaning of victory. No one promised that life would be one long gala event, but if we're made of durable stuff, we neither let it hinder us nor make us run roughshod to get ahead.

We must always recognize past hardships for what they are.

We cannot ignore them, for they are a part of our makeup. But neither can we let them become crutches to lean upon when there's need for an excuse.

Bitterness over past experiences wastes valuable time. Perhaps it was those hardships that gave us the strength to rise above the mediocre things. However crude, ugly or unhappy, even tragic, some of the times may seem, as seen alone, when combined with all our other knowledge they form the perfect circle and play no more important part than all the rest.

In the words of American poet John Neal, "No man ever worked his passage anywhere in a dead calm."

Think on pleasant things. Deliberately turn your thoughts to something pleasant when the pressures are too intense. And be careful as undisciplined thought quickly sifts back to the unhappy, unsettled mind.

The greater part of the time we are victims of our emotions. They play havoc with our peace of mind and are great friends of pessimism. They tell us things are true with such sincerity that we believe them into fact. They convince us things are a certain way and that we cannot remedy them with any amount of effort.

But stop where you are and consider what it is you are listening to and how it affects your feelings. Do a turn-about and take the positive route of deliberately replacing thoughts of unhappinesses, injustices, and misunderstandings with the thought that these are merely chariots to carry us past all that has withheld freedom.

Until you've walked in the rain you cannot truly appreciate the protection of shelter.

Unless you've felt the heat from a sweltering sun you cannot fully enjoy the coolness of shade.

Only after the clatter and bang of crowded places can you find quietness and solitude so soothing to the nerves.

Before you can stop worrying and start living, there must be an elimination of fear which is the cause of all worry.

Sometimes, unfortunately, we must collide with the bad before we can totally appreciate the good.

It is sad that we too often must be reminded of our obligations before we take charge of them.

Frequently it seems we must have our freedom threatened before we muster enough patriotism to defend it.

Too many shoulders are bowed by our thoughtlessness before we finally learn the key to real success is kindness.

We never know how truly wonderful it is to be loved until we are after we've failed to deserve it.

M. R. Smith's words, "God's plans, like lilies pure and white untold—We must not tear the close shut leaves apart—Time will reveal the calyxes of gold," reveal, after all, that patience does its perfect work.

When you hear geese honking their way southward in the quiet of the night, when you hear hunters' guns in the woods, and church bells ringing through the crystal clear autumn air, then you've heard the sounds of Thanksgiving.

Perhaps memories of Thanksgiving are not the same for everyone. Each carries his own within his heart, and some live only for past Thanksgivings when a family was more complete. And so this day serves only to remind them of happier times. Those times should be remembered in all their glory and yet, there is the now. It is important too. Perhaps in some ways it is more important, for the challenge to quit thinking of ourselves and to consider how sorely needed is every last person. How memorable we could make this day for someone who hasn't even a happy memory. How strong one can be, not for themselves, but for that memory and for those who do not have the strength.

Some young child or some young adult may be looking for a pattern to go by, some reason to be truly thankful, and here is the opportunity.

Some of our most delightful hours are spent in conversation with those people sometimes known as senior citizens, our elders, and lovingly grandmother or grandfather. But whatever their titles they still have a wealth of wisdom and experience to share with us.

Whether we accept the experiences of our elders to profit by, or if we choose to ignore them, will determine a great deal on how alert and aware we are of life. For this is life, this experience, this knowledge.

And within these lives we find so many things, small though they may be, that have a great part to play in our success or failure as human beings and parents. For they have learned what still remains sacred in man's heart, though years may pass and times may change.

To most the unhappy times are forgotten. And left to live are the beautiful beloved things that work as well today as yesterday. Things like cheerfulness, and refusal to take unpleasantness as final; a warm and friendly kitchen where guests had rather be, and a Bible well read; a shining faith and a belief that the impossible only takes a little longer; and, a good broad shoulder to catch our tears—And love, which after all was the beginning of all of this.

It takes such a little whiff of memory to carry us all the way back. Small things tucked here and there remind us of some place, some thing, some person who has played a special part in our lives.

We want to go forward, try new things, know new people, visit new places, yet how nice to slip on those comfortable old slippers of the familiar by-gones and remember loving faces and happy times.

It is said that we should never return to places that have a sacred spot in our memories. Everything changes with time, so little remains recognizable to us. We begin to think that perhaps those hallowed places were not so wonderful as we remember.

71

But they were, for in their time and that place it was as it should have been, happy and meaningful. They may have changed, but so have we.

A little of every place and every person goes with us in the building of even happier times. We have not lost anyone or anything but it is the combination of all that we have lived and learned that builds our character and teaches us the way of life.

Whenever we stop to consider where we are on the road of life, we might also think about why we are there. Whether it is success or failure, or wavering in the middle of the road, we are where we are because of someone or some thing.

Nearly every person can pinpoint the time in their life when there was a turning point, a change for worse or for the better. And usually there is someone to whom they give the credit for such a change.

Throughout our lives we contact many people, and they each leave an impression. As living continues the combination of all those thoughts and feelings and actions forms our opinions, our likes and dislikes, our fears and our loves. But there is one basic factor in all of this that turns us one way or the other—the individual, the personal self. It is how we take life, what we expect, how we do our daily tasks, where we place our values that makes the difference.

We are born with the right to choose—and whatever we choose there will always be someone there to help us be good or bad. But first, we must give credit where credit is due.

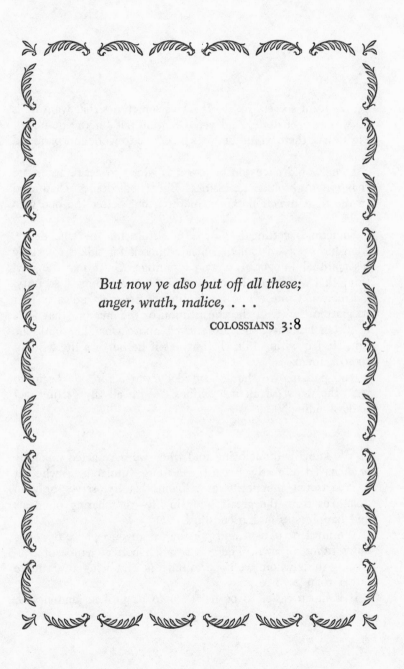

But now ye also put off all these;
anger, wrath, malice, . . .

COLOSSIANS 3:8

We want so very much. It seems sometimes that wanting is all we ever get done. And yet if it were not for the desires of our hearts, there would be little incentive to work and plan and expect.

Some would have you believe it is wrong to desire any more than your absolute necessities. But good desires channeled in the right direction can do nothing but better the one who seeks.

Sometimes getting is only a substitute for the true desire. Man has a way of looking outside himself for things to satisfy his spiritual hunger. It may be prestige. Or it may be anything that will inflate his ego and give him a feeling of security.

Emerson wrote, "The implanting of a desire indicates that its gratification is in the constitution of the creature that feels it." Man has the ability to rise far above what he thinks he can. He has within him the answers if he but has the wisdom to seek them.

And perhaps we should consider, even before we begin to seek, the wisest of all instructions, "With all thy getting, get understanding."

We know without being told when we have acted unkindly or behaved unjustly toward someone. Intolerance, whether it is personal superiority or religious bigotry, serves only to isolate us from the greatest joy in life—the sharing of ideals and happinesses and friendships.

We must be patient and fair toward anyone whose opinions differ from our own. There is a much better chance of convincing those whom we hope to influence by being an example rather than a voice.

It is much easier to be led than to be pushed, and not so

hard to be tolerant when we recognize within ourselves the reasons we are not always tolerant.

It sometimes becomes habitual to be dissatisfied with everything we see others do. We don't take time to understand and know the basis for their actions. We often fall short of listening to them long enough to understand, and their next words or actions may explain it.

We cannot afford to be intolerant, because no matter how good our ideas are, there is always a better one!

Bad feelings are only burdens. When we get to the point of believing the whole world is sour because we don't understand it, we have a lot of self-searching to do. Maybe we helped to lose its sweetness. Maybe we're the bad apple that soured the whole lot.

Our first thought should be to make amends. Sometimes we can't, and when such is the case we need to get out of the way and let time and nature take its course.

Life is too beautiful to go on being a bitter pill that insists that everyone swallow it. As in the words of Caleb C. Colton, an English clergyman around the turn of the century, "The man who has so little knowledge of human nature as to seek happiness by changing anything but his own dispositions, will waste his life in fruitless efforts, and multiply the grief which he proposes to remove."

We need to unburden ourselves by forgetting ourselves and doing something that will put a smile on someone else's face.

The quickest way to solve the problem of hurt feelings is to inquire if this situation is important to the whole existence. Does this particular thing mean more than any of the other things of life? It is amazing how quickly trials fade into nothingness when faced with this question. It places before the individual the need to decide here and now the meaning of his whole existence.

There are not many things in our lives that we can truthfully say mean everything to us. The small things are important

75

and very dear, but the really significant things we count on one hand—life, our loved ones, our good desires and our faith and our nation.

One of the most magnified situations in this day is taking life too seriously. In the stress of too much mental confusion we seem unable to laugh off so many little irritations. We let personality rule us into making each little problem the source of great anxiety and dramatically lay hold of it until it chokes us.

The worthwhile side of this life is too important to let ourselves become involved with things that mean little to us. Too much of the trouble in the world is caused from ego-building importance that would never be missed in anyone's existence.

If you don't know what to do about a situation—wait awhile, the answer will come. If weariness overcomes you before you've completed a difficult job, wait awhile, you'll get your second wind.

If you do not agree with someone else's philosophy, don't fret, perhaps later you will come to know that the same philosophy can be reached from many different directions.

If you think the activities of another person or group are frivolous and unnecessary, wait a bit, they most likely will feel the same way about you sometime.

If you don't like what someone else has to say, wait, he may clarify it—or you may change your mind.

If life hasn't dished you up a lot of happiness, wait a bit, if you've planted any happiness seeds you will also reap.

We can't always wait, but sometimes waiting is action, and action of the hardest kind. It is difficult to keep quiet when you've something to say, but it more often saves your face later and sometimes your life.

Do you remember the interesting story of the lion and the mouse in Aesop's Fables? The lion could have crushed the mouse but was merciful and let him go free. A year later the lion became entangled and the mouse nibbled her way through the net to set him free.

It is a dangerous thing to wade through other people's feelings, burning our bridges and believing we will never need them again. The saddest person on earth must be the one who finds he has tried to destroy the only one who can help him.

The smallest and seemingly most insignificant has a purpose in this world, and it isn't for us to judge what that purpose is. We have enough to do in finding our own.

As in the fable, we must remember, "Few are so small or weak, I guess . . . but may assist us in distress . . . nor shall we ever . . . if we're wise . . . the meanest of the least despise."

Regret is something everyone has, but no one can afford to keep. Being remorseful is commendable when we should be sorry for wrong behavior, but to live with regret is to add to it day by day. There are those who are unable to admit they have ever been wrong. But there are more who carry with them so much regret they are bowed in spirit.

Thomas Moore, the Irish poet, once said, "Remorse is beholding heaven and feeling hell," but perhaps just knowing heaven can exist makes regret more hellish. And so often it renders the regretful almost powerless to lift himself of his predicament.

But there is forgiveness! A daily vow or affirmation can take us a step further in lifting ourselves above the things that cause regret. And if we've settled down in the middle of unhappiness to enjoy our lot in life, then, moment by moment, inch by inch, we shall overcome that, too!

Have you noticed how hardheaded we are about clinging to the one way we think something should be done? If it worked once, we think it should again, and perhaps it does. There are proven methods of getting successful results in many things.

77

But ever so often we try to use the same procedure, follow the same general pattern we've used before, only this time it doesn't work.

How we pound our fists against that stone wall! Insisting all the time that there used to be a door in exactly that spot. Who moved the door? Frequently circumstances are to blame. But placing the blame is not the important thing. Finding the way is important.

The way may not be marked plainly, and we have to blaze a new trail, find a new method. But the hardest part of finding that new method is in admitting we need one. The first and most important step is in changing our idea of how it should be done. As soon as we have accepted this fact the mind has a reserve of experiences and knowledge that will hurry in to help. But only after we've admitted the need for it.

It has been said that hell hath no fury like a woman scorned. But it is even truer that there is no hell more furious than any human being who feels scorn within himself for himself. It is natural but painful for anyone who does not know the meaning of love to find fault and grief within his own existence. Unable to accept the blame for his actions, there is a continual search for the cause in other people.

How can we tell what point in life someone may have reached in his development? We can only see and sense the pain that some carry while they learn the way. If it is impossible to get along with them, we should get along without them, but condemning them will never turn the tide.

Understanding of others and of ourselves has been a great human need for all time. The fact that we do not look with a critical eye, pecking away in constant irritation at someone's faults, but give some sign of friendliness, some patience for rebellious spirits, may serve as the turning point for him. And to try for such understanding does no harm for the one who makes the effort.

"Though we speak with the tongues of men and angels and give our bodies to be burned, if we are irritable or hard to live with, it all accounts for nothing," wrote Margaret Widdemer.

Wouldn't it be a blessing to ourselves and to others if we could be as gentle and considerate in temper as we expect others to be? It is not a good thing to keep pent up the emotions that rule us so continually, but neither is it good to be too quick and too constantly blowing off steam.

It may serve as a tension reliever to us, but it can soon ruin our relationships with others. And without our realizing it, we can soon become a chronic complainer.

Worry, physical ailments and weariness can cause a short temper that we think others should understand. And most have a way of knowing if that is the case, but prolonged impositions on other people will wear that tolerance very thin. It takes two to have an argument, but it takes only one to start it.

The need to forgive and to be forgiven should never be overlooked. To pass over a disagreement quickly without thought to the damage we've done can take the shine off any friendship. There can be no merit in forgetting if we cannot first forgive.

There are two voices in this world that will be forever unpopular. One is the voice of self-pity, the other the voice that yells all the time. One declares itself to be the victim of great injustice, the other yells to demand justice.

The person who believes himself to be the victim of injustice —one who believes he is "meant to suffer"—will always find conditions to prove he was right.

And the one who yells, "Look what I've sacrificed," and always with the theme, "What I've tried to do for you," has slowed another's progress and stopped his own.

A true victim of circumstances is easily recognized, and does not care to be noticed as such. And the one who yells his merits has received his reward, so there isn't another.

Both have their attentions turned inward, but to the sorrow of most . . . their voices are not.

True forgiveness could be described as a "divine amnesty" where we receive a pardon from the unworthy things we've done, and have another chance to prove our worth. Forgiveness is something we must give in order to receive. And we have a tendency to linger over old grudges, using them to bolster our reason for not forgiving. But we cannot return to the past, nor can we change one whit of anything that happened then. We cannot make up for resentments we've caused in others, no more than they can make up for ours.

To forgive is divine. God is above punishment, but we are not. It is we, not God, who punish by taking things into our own hands and making them work for our own selfish reasons. We demand punishment by hanging on to painful past experiences that produce self-pity. We are the ones who blame God's will for our illnesses, our poverty, our lack of friends. But we are wrong, for there is a moment of truth when we face ourselves and know that we are the guilty.

And there is a time such as William Wordsworth wrote about, ". . . that blessed mood, in which the burden of the mystery, in which the heavy and weary weight of all this unintelligible world, is lightened" . . . because we've been forgiven.

Hardly any of us are without some jealousy. We like to think of ourselves above that painful emotion, because such a monstrous feeling is a destructive thing. But if we have not felt a normal amount of it, it is because we have yet to doubt something we love very much.

Margaret, Queen of Navarre, and sister of Francis I, King of France in the fifteenth century, wrote the following words:

"Love may exist without jealousy, although this is rare; but jealousy may exist without love, and that is common; for jealousy can feed on that which is bitter, no less than on that which is sweet, and is sustained by pride as often as by affection."

Jealousy can rear its head when logic is giving you the facts, and throw the whole thing into chaos. But confidence is the enemy of jealousy. Confidence, trust and faith are all strong parts of a nature where jealousy does not rule.

And jealousy, even in moderation, can introduce us to a serious problem with ourselves, if we let it grow out of proportion. It breeds rejection while maturity and understanding keep us safely within the bounds of permissiveness rather than possessiveness.

The destructive hand is one that never finds a friendly one to shake. Its finger is always pointed to someone in an accusation. It is shaking in someone's face in a threat. The destructive hand is forever lifted against anyone who differs, ready to strike in disagreement, always lifted for attention to let them tell the wrong someone has done.

The destructive hand tries desperately to hold another's good back . . . ready to sign a complaint . . . forever in a gesture of disdain.

But pity for the destructive hand. It will never know the tenderness of love nor find the clasp of friendship. It will never feel the sun warm on its palm while it lifts someone . . . or guide another to happier things . . . or to wave or cheer or to praise and give thanks.

The destructive hand is the negative approach to all of life. It can never do anything but discourage and frighten. The positive approach to life is found in every gesture of the productive hand; it builds unbreakable structures, unbroken peace, and joy to soothe the most savage heart.

Don't allow life to mean too much. Keep it light and shallow for easy treading; spend as much time as possible scoffing at those things meaningful to others; forget the decency and patience in their attitudes.

And look with overbearing revenge to make them pay for

81

what they believe . . . laugh at their efforts . . . call attention to their imperfections . . . and don't forget to learn how to live alone . . . if not in body, then in spirit. And then don't take the blame for a desert-island soul. It is of one's own making. But remember, oh so well, that life does not stand still while we search for someone to blame for our isolation.

There must be a great many persons who have questioned their own wisdom in having fought for a principle. To so many, it seems all they gleaned from it was the title "different." Isn't this why so many refuse too much to stand up for what they believe? We look at them in disbelief, the idea that someone is trying to attract attention. If they are not twitted about their actions they are treated with cold indifference, which can be even worse.

It seems that if a person has the strength to say he will fight for a certain truth, he must also have the strength to fight alone. That is, until everyone looks at everyone else to see how they should conform and will not be embarrassed or counted as unusual to follow this particular thought.

But he who finds himself alone in the stand he takes must remember that if it is truth he is following it will eventually win and at least he can live with himself. Not everyone can say that.

H. W. Beecher has written, "It is often said it is no matter what a man believes if he is only sincere. But let a man sincerely believe that seed planted without ploughing is as good as with; that January is as favorable for seed-sowing as April; and that cockle seed will produce as good a harvest as wheat, and is it so?"

Where do we stand? If a man is sincere in his beliefs should we never try to inspire him otherwise? There is no one more dedicated and more sincere than a Communist. No one could have been more sincere than our wartime enemies, and in these we can see that sincerity alone cannot always be good.

Sincerity, like trust, must be rooted in those basic truths

that are for the good of everyone. If that which we sincerely believe in and live by is truly good, then the results will speak so loudly that all who really want to will see. Until man sincerely wants to know good and do good, he will never know it. And until he does he only half lives.

The truly humble person is one who has no thought of "using" other people to his own avail. He is aware that any success he may attain comes not entirely from his own intelligence and abilities, but because somewhere along the way he has acknowledged how inadequate he is alone.

The day of the self sufficient person has never truly been. Without other people, without a sense of humility, success is lost to the overambitious.

English critic John Ruskin once said that the first test of a truly great man is his humility.

There is greatness and sincerity when a person can say to himself that he is only human and except for the grace of God he would even lack those qualities. He realizes that the world owes him nothing, and no man owes him anything but love. It is not simply the other person's job to serve him, but it is his duty to serve others.

Humility is one of the finest qualities found in man. Without it he is nothing but a brash machine, with it he is warm and kind and always respected.

If you want to be a friend of man, meet him on his level. This isn't to say you have to be the type he is, but understand him and realize that it is a good thing that everyone is not alike. This is the beauty of humanity, the variations that keep the human race from being monotonous.

And there is nothing sweeter to the human ear than to hear someone talk his language. Great men have realized this and have made themselves adaptable to the little and to the big, to the learned and to the unschooled, in order to be more widely understood.

Who knew better than the Wise Master the importance of

meeting man on his own level? As He looked into the lives of every type of person He saw many changes that needed to be made, but He also saw much to love and to waken. And in this gentleness and compassion He could meet every man and speak his language, then to be understood and followed.

We live such narrow existences when we cannot communicate with anyone except those on our own level of thought and action. And if we only have one level on which to operate, there's danger of it becoming a shelf for immovable objects.

Human dignity is that silent something in man that keeps him from falling below the level where others look down on him to make light of his very existence. There isn't a human being who cannot sense to some degree the feeling that others have for him. It may create in him a "show them" attitude that takes him through life more successfully, but it will more likely destroy his desire to be anything more than what is expected of him.

It is an appalling thing to see someone impose his superiority upon the human dignity of those whose literacy may not be equal to his own. Only profound ignorance could convince anyone he had the right to see and idly judge another's intelligence, or to insult the dignity of any man.

The little silent people who have not yet discovered within themselves the abilities they need to lift themselves, still have the right and dignity of being human. A small amount of respect and direction might start them on the road to better things, though it might be all uphill. At least, if he knows it is all uphill he may work harder and reach a place where he can look back at those with lofty ideas about themselves, standing forever stagnant, and feel more compassion than they could ever have felt.

There is much to be said of small things. Even in this age of emphasis on "bigness" we must realize that bigness is only a

84

mass of small things. An idea is a small thing. With it we can change our world. We can take a tiny seed and give it careful attention and reap a hundredfold. We can take a little idea and give it our careful attention and build it into a fortune.

A smile is a small thing. Smile once at someone in passing and three will return the smile. Smiling is so contagious that it moves from person to person until a hundred smiling faces are the result of one.

A thought is a small thing. One thought inspires another and another until a mental image is formed. From that mental image blueprints are drawn. And from those blueprints worlds are built.

Hope is a small thing. One tiny glimmer of hope can lift us out of the deepest pit of darkness. One whisper of encouragement will help us to know that as long as there's hope there is an excellent chance.

A wish is a small thing. Like a little prayer, it climbs the steps to an idea that makes a smile and gives us hope to make our wishes come true. For in small things are all great things formed, in little beginnings the possibilities of great events.

Charity never faileth: . . .

I CORINTHIANS 13:8

There may be many reasons why man wants to conquer the world, but there is something youthful and soul-stirring to be able to do it for somebody. Living within oneself is barren and shallow, lacking in warmth and without understanding. But when we can be outgoing and giving, the importance of others becomes doubly strong.

It is impossible to even be selfish without the help of others. Who would we take from, blame troubles on, resent, and criticize? But more important, who would care when we're ill, who would be happy when we're blessed, and who would love us when we least deserve it?

The world may be deluged with problems and solutions, laws to live by, formulas, fear, faith and the everlasting struggle to survive in the face of others, but it is just as necessary to share laughter in happiness, to know God in a sunset, and to feel joy in a sunrise, all more beautiful because of others.

Victor Hugo wrote that the greatest happiness in life is in knowing that others love us, for ourselves, or rather, they love us in spite of ourselves.

"I owe no man anything but love" it is said. But what is love? Love is duty—whatever duty may require to accomplish a good thing.

Love is peace. One must not only be peaceful but contribute to the peace of others. Let there be peace and let it begin with me.

Love is sometimes pain. We must give up something that causes us pain because it is for the good of the greatest number.

Love is understanding. That others do not have to forever explain their actions to us. That we know their reasons without being told.

Love is courage. Courage to lead where one has the ability to lead. Courage to stand up for what one believes in and wants to live.

Love is faith. Faith in God, faith in self and faith in others. Everyone is not above reproach, but we must have faith that the majority strives to be.

Coleridge wrote, "He prayeth best who loveth best," which seems to rule out all hollow and self-heard prayers. For a person who truly loves does not hear himself only, or rule all life useless because he cannot love or pray.

Life can be as simple as love and prayer. Where the two mingle there can be no jealousy, resentment or fear.

Jealousy makes us compare our lot with another's. And there can be no comparison, for no two people are alike.

Resentment plunges an otherwise logical soul into despair and an endless journey of revenge.

And fear rushes us headlong into situations that detract, accidents that could be prevented, and long delays in reaching our goals.

But if we can, for a few moments, invite into our hearts a thing called love, then we can pray. And if we can pray we have the source of all answers to our aid.

Irritation, they say, is something gentle folk should never know. Always passive, they go along the way smiling, no matter what the cost to feelings. But have you ever tried to smile when all the street lights are red and someone honked loudly when you failed to move quickly enough.

Have you heard a politician slur the name of your candidate . . . and had a promise broken without so much as a faint explanation. Or perhaps the long explanations on how to do something you've done for years . . . and suddenly you want to make two lists for people you like and people you don't like!

And maybe you've answered the telephone and heard them hang up simply because your voice was not the right voice. . . .

Or had them stand back empty handed while you with your packages opened the door for them?

Well, it's no easy matter to be gentle folk and the mildest can get warm all over again by just thinking of an injustice. Perhaps it is trifling to let such little things irritate. But the best of us feel it. Small things that we never quite get over sometimes. We forgive and forget except to think about it occasionally, and then we must consider the words of Seneca, "Anger, if not restrained, is frequently more hurtful to us than the injury that provokes it."

We live in a continual round of adjustments. It is usually an admirable thing to be able to make adjustments easily. Not many can. And, yet, it makes us wonder at times if those who can so freely change and move without emotions have ever felt very deeply.

We tend to cling to familiar things, familiar customs. There is a great security in traveling a way we know by heart. The roughest road can usually be traveled without incident when we know every turn and bump.

It has been said by those who do scientific research that it takes at least three weeks to adjust to changes. But three months would do it more justice. And it must be done by abandonment, by setting aside for a period of time all things like the old way. Many times it is done not for ourselves alone, for it is foolish to believe a change involves only ourselves.

In our very complex way of life there is no situation to affect only one person. And often the most wonderful thing we can do for someone else is to find our own balance by making adjustments quickly, even in the middle of chaos.

Everyone is a collector of something. And everyone's collection looks peculiar to someone else. And yet, who knows why an item may have a certain appeal to one particular person. The shape, the color, the whole idea may have a hidden background, but it is most definitely there!

It may be old books, or magazines. Perhaps it is pill bottles, fishing hooks, or something "I may need someday when . . ." Who knows the reason old calendars continue to hang, and scraps of this and that may someday be just what I need.

But more dear than any of these are the happy thoughts we collect to use along the way. We can use them to cheer someone, to pass along a word of courage, a simple prayer, a smile. And when someone has time to share with us an experience that we may profit by the pain they felt—yes, these are collector's items. These priceless bits of life's fabric, woven by someone's cares and offered to us in hopes that it will help.

Whatever it is that we collect, we must never forget the dearest collections are the kindnesses, the thoughtful acts, the smiling faces that can be ours by giving the same.

What could be so priceless as true friendship? Friends for which time and space do not exist! It is written, "What a great blessing is a friend with breast so trusty that thou mayest safely bury all thy secrets in it, whose conscience thou mayest fear less than thy own; who can relieve thy cares by his conversation, thy doubts by his counsels, thy sadness by his good humor, and whose very looks give thee comfort."

All of us have had many friends, but the special ones remain forever in our memories. The dearest are those who believe in us and are willing to trust us with their friendship.

We cannot force friendship. It is something mutually felt, mutually understood and silently accepted. It is our opportunity to demonstrate our very best selves—to ask no questions and to pass no criticisms.

"Before us is a future all unknown, a path untrod;
Beside us a friend well loved and known—
That friend is God."

Have you heard how dreadful the neighbors are these days to ignore another's plight, and how the world has gone to the dogs because people don't care? Have you heard how hardened hearts are and how callous and unfeeling the human race has become?

91

It may be true such things do happen . . . for we hear about it daily. But it likely is that we hear more about the unusual than the usual.

For have you heard about the builder who laid his own plans aside to help another build his house . . . and the lady who gave her home and nursing care to someone who had no other place to go. Or the child who found its needs fulfilled in the love of a foster mother.

We may ignore, but we can never erase the love of the human race for the human race. The world may abound with sordid happenings; it may revel in senseless activities. But called to help, the greater number will respond without thought of the cost to them.

Of these things we hear so little. With these we come in contact every day and accept it as the normal pattern of life . . . which it is . . . for each unthinking, infantile mind there are two great thoughtful ones. And the second great Commandment still works its wonders in the lives of men.

We are all aware of the emotional effect color creates. And for this reason we choose colors that please the eye by first pleasing the inner emotions. Certain colors have the same effect on many, while other colors affect each of us individually and in particular ways.

Red has an exciting effect; green is cool serenity, orange is the color of vivacity, and brown tones are restful earthy colors. People dress to enhance their appearances with certain colors. Homes are decorated and offices are planned to create pleasant surroundings.

And we as individuals possess moods of many colors. Yet, we are far more careless about the color of that mood, letting the attitudes and colors of others dictate to us how we are to behave. If we could remember when we meet someone whose mood is black, to remind ourselves that his mood is his own, there would be less involvement in the emotions of others.

We are so vividly aware of color, we must not be reckless

in recognizing the color scheme within our own personality. Whether it be a vibrant color, sophisticated, or bright and witty, color always works its subtle magic.

If everyone were alike, what a dull world this would be. It is the individuality of each person that makes the world so interesting.

The tremendous differences in people give a wide range of personalities, beliefs and appearances to every group, no matter how small.

If all the flowers in the world were of one color, would we think them so beautiful? It is the variety and wide range of rainbow colors that keeps us fascinated.

Cowper wrote, "Variety is the very spice of life, that gives it all its flavor." So many have no thought of life except what they will eat, what they will wear and how they can entertain themselves. And then we come on someone who has the ability to see loveliness in the sunlight and charm in quiet rain. They can say things to encourage, or to make calm and peaceful.

In our lives, we meet many different kinds of people. Some we love and some we like and love, which is a terrific difference. It is to find a wholeness or a part of our lost self in someone else. It isn't that they are so much like us or that we believe the way they do, but that they communicate, and it is this rare communication that respects the difference between peoples.

So often it is difficult to know where the line lies between kindness and domineering. It doesn't sound as if the two could possibly mix, but sometimes in our watchfulness over those we care about we're inclined to think it a kind of goodness when it actually becomes domineering.

It is often the best and kindest thing to let someone else think for himself. Even though the helpfulness is of love, it can be smothering to the one who wants to breathe freely, even of his own problems.

Concern can turn to possessiveness in the space of a moment and do it so subtly it is almost impossible to comprehend. Every person has the right to make his own mistakes and also the undeniable right to correct them. It makes help appreciated when it comes and then help is recognized as help and not as ownership.

If every person should be told what to do, it would relieve him of the burden of the responsibility of thinking, planning or making decisions. His life would be literally free of care. And there are those who love to direct the traffic of other people's lives. But have you noticed how detestable it is to them to have the smallest suggestion made concerning their own? What a rare display of vanity!

There are always sycophants, or "apple polishers," if you will, who fawn and flatter the vanity. But to have one's vanity built to great heights is not always an act of love, but more often subtle scorn.

Love is the only force against vanity. Love does not wish to command, but only to serve. If love cannot tell the truth it does not speak. Vanity separates, love joins. Love does not ask that another take the responsibility, but it asks only the strength to bear it.

There always seems to be one person in every society who feels it his duty to read the riot act to whomever, in his opinion, is in need of it at the moment. Come be my friend until I have time to let you know the things you're doing wrong. This is a committee of one, in all my busy days . . . taking time to straighten out all who are not conforming to my ideas.

Who, in all the world, has so much wisdom as to consider themselves so forever right . . . to be capable of such certainty as to what another person should do. And even if they should be right, who commissioned them in all their wisdom to speak the words that have such power to wither a spirit.

94

When the world has so much hurt, why should one voice be raised against another who has not spoken an unkind word in his direction. When even the strongest is so in need of compassion and love, why is one voice, sharp edged and driven deep, allowed to speak.

Our words can build or destroy. And we never really know just when something we say may make a decision for someone else, to give them courage or further fear. But God help all who have not learned the words we speak come back to us . . . many times.

So much has been written about happiness, the way to it, the reasons for it, the symbols of it, and still people search for that very special something that will assure happiness forever after. Of all the recipes for lasting happiness, we finally have to mix our own. But the one thing everyone has in common is the need for a little bit more. We have this and this, for which we are very thankful, but always the need is extended to that little bit more.

Happiness is like any other part of our lives, we must use wisdom in seeking it. We too often rush headlong into something that seems to be instant happiness, all the time telling ourselves we can right the wrong at a later time. But happiness doesn't remain happiness for very long when it has such strings attached.

In order to be rightly happy we concentrate on getting, but it is giving that we find most necessary to mix into every recipe. To some happiness will always be elusive, never quite settling anywhere, never quite revealing itself, for they have yet to learn that happiness has the wings of angels, the breath of God, and the love of man, all hidden within himself.

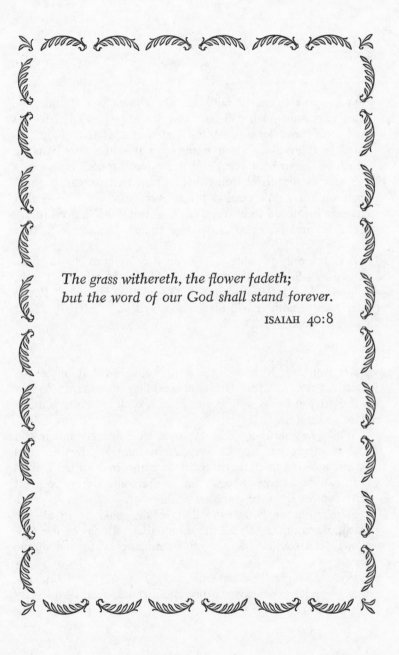

The grass withereth, the flower fadeth;
but the word of our God shall stand forever.

ISAIAH 40:8

You speak to me of faith and the church you attend. The most important faith will be the way you feel about it within you. Don't ever let anyone tell you that it is too unsophisticated to think about such things. For it is the very basis on which you draw your breath. Without faith there's no hope.

The most beautiful thing about life is that we can begin it anew each day. We need to forget every unpleasant thing that has ever happened to us, every shallow thing that has no meaning, every unkind word or deed or thought and start all over again.

And the only possible way to do it is by faith. Faith, faith in yourself, faith in others, faith in God, and faith that right will win. And facetiously stated, "Them that has, gits." If you have a little faith it will attract more—if you feel right about it within you.

Do you want to know the truth about worry? It hits everyone. It is not an ailment just for weaklings or cowards. Worry is the cat you throw out only to have it back in before you can close the door.

Worry has another side. It proves we care very much and that we appreciate our God-given gifts and loved ones. In a way, it is a sign of strength, for if we can turn it to faith, then faith can be just as strong. And to overcome worry, or to at least control it, there must be faith.

Faith, and the knowledge that if you could be in all the places, watching closely all the things about which you are concerned, you couldn't do a tenth as much good as one simple prayer.

We are taught, "Be not anxious," "Fear not" and "Be not afraid," and too quickly we become anxious, fearful and very frightened. But even then we have only to put worry to flight by remembering those quieting words that are so absolutely true, "Be still and know that I am God."

Recently we had a summer storm. It was rumbling and heavy with darkness. The lightning flashed across the sky, and trees bent back and forth in the uncertain currents. When the first huge drops of rain spattered across the walks and lawns, our thoughts turned to the safety of anyone or anything that might be caught out in the wind and rain.

We've been through many summer storms. Some of them left permanent marks upon our memories. The threatening, the darkness, the pressure of the atmosphere are not so different from the emotional storms of the human life. We see lives under pressure bend to and fro in the uncertainty of life. We know concern for the safety of those who experience emotional storms. Then we know the only answer is in God's hands. There is no other way.

The good earth rights herself quickly after a storm. Nature comes forth more richly for having gone through the storm, and the scars are lost in new growth. And blessed are we when we lift ourselves up to a new, deeper radiance and peace.

To have the desire to quit in the face of despair is not a new story. As long as time, people have wanted to give up when something hindered their progress. But such adversity is sometimes the right time for man to become acquainted with himself.

It has been written that a smooth sea does not make a skillful mariner. The storms of human life like those of the seas awaken us to sharpening our abilities and strengthening us to overcome these present storms to the point where we seldom have to face them again. Most of living is a lesson, and the sooner we learn to study and develop the sooner we are rid of the teacher.

But in the words of Jeremy Taylor, "It is impossible for that man to despair who remembers that his Helper is omnipotent."

99

And it is impossible for man not to progress if he acknowledges his Helper in the most minute detail of his life.

Prepared for the worst? Forget it! Only worry prepares for the worst. If problems come to you, meet them with courage when they arrive. And worry has never produced courage. Faith produces courage, and keeps us from crossing all those unnecessary bridges. In fact, we cross bridges that have never been in existence, and have no strength except that which we give them by constant preparation for something that isn't good.

Promise yourself to cross no bridges this day except those you find immediately before you. And nine times out of ten they will lead only to happiness.

The longest face and the saddest cry
Always seem to come with the question why
Why did you take what belonged to me?
It has always been mine, or can't you see
That you have no rights, no right to claim,
And you did just that, you're to blame
For all my unhappiness, all of my tears.
Well, perhaps not all, part were my fears.
And I suppose if I think I can also say
That if I've lost anything, it's really the way
That I treated the things that used to be mine.
I saw clouds on the days where there was really sunshine,
I turned often to darkness instead of the light.
I saw all of the wrong, but never the right,
And in all honesty I suppose I must say
If I've lost anything, I gave it away.

If you could remake your personal world, how would you want it? Very few can answer that question immediately. Many cannot answer after a great deal of consideration. Perhaps all of us are drifters to a degree. There seems to be a certain amount of apprehension and fear about saying, or even thinking of what we want out of life. It may be that we feel some of it isn't right to want, or that maybe we are asking more than should be our share.

Money is probably the first thing that most people think about, because of what they could do for themselves and for others. But what of health and peace and love? Without these all the fame and money in the world would be entirely meaningless. Without a spiritual foundation to one's life, all our desires are built on sand. Without knowing where we're going, we are drifters.

To know what we want with good purpose is the first and most important step. As Carlyle wrote, "The man without a purpose is like a ship without a rudder—a waif, a nothing. Have a purpose in life, and, having it, throw such strength of mind and muscle into your work as God has given you."

Tennyson wrote these beautiful words: "More things are wrought by prayer than this world dreams of. What are men better than sheep or goats, that nourish a blind life within the brain, if, knowing God, they lift no hands of prayer both for themselves and those who call them friends!"

What on this earth could we possibly have of good that has not come from the Almighty? What inroads are made into disease and sickness, what light has focused more understandingly on mental illness and weaknesses, without having been revealed through something greater than we are?

And indeed, to what can we contribute the smallest or the greatest amounts of success, the love we share, the true joys, the peace, and our very breath. How presumptuous of man to believe he owns one thing of lasting value that does not come from God.

Aim high, even though it seems at the moment you'll never reach that cherished dream. It is the duty of man to lift himself above mediocrity. And if you're afraid your dream would sound foolish, then don't talk about it, work for it.

Some dreams have gossamer wings, too fragile to discuss. We can be so zealous about our plans that we talk away the mystery and lose interest in the things we've begun. Zeal can burn itself out in one, quick, bright flame, or it can be nurtured into strength that is the basis for greatness.

If dreams have substance, then they may well come true. And if they are in line with the law of good, then there will be someone who wants to help. To have the desire to do something that will benefit others, the desire to serve, is to have a dream with solid possibilities.

The aims, then, must be deserving as to become duties. It befalls certain ones to develop a gift and to use it in helping other people. As German philosopher Immanuel Kant has written, "What are the aims which are at the same time duties? They are the perfecting of ourselves and the happiness of others."

Courage must have its everyday face. We can't preserve it just for special occasions. We must have courage when we are disappointed, because disappointment is a robber of reason and faith, and even dignity. We must remember that whatever we have to meet there is something within us to help us meet it. But it is like a vein of rich ore. We must tap it, know what it is, and turn it into a finished product that will serve a purpose.

Every day we must have courage to forgive. The adamant we shall always face, but to forgive is to disarm. To forgive is to release and to release is to remove the graceless things that make it necessary to forgive.

A little common, everyday courage can give a life so much more to live for and to find contentment in the knowledge that today I did not give in to the smaller self. And I can draw on the strength from One who bore personal suffering with supreme courage.

A comforting old adage is that it is always darkest just before the dawn. The darkness of fear and worry and misunderstanding can last only so long, and then the light of dawn breaks through to show everything in its true perspective.

To someone who is troubled, the darkness holds only the most frightening difficulties. This kind of night seems to have no end, but given a little time it will pass, as will our problems.

The very fact that we are not alone should give some comfort, for no matter what we are experiencing someone else has been there too. We must not delude ourselves with notions that we are meant to be cross-bearers forever.

And frequently, it is a much better person who emerges from his own night to remember that it is as important to have faith in the dark as it is easy to have faith in the sunshine.

Why is it that the things we love can cause us so much pain, and perhaps without realizing it? Why is it that we find so much to worry about in all the "what if's" that cross our minds with such persistence? What makes fatigue follow us through the hours and drain away precious strength that we need to help us in our daily routine?

All the things that plague us daily have one common cause —fear. To some, fear is a constant companion. He may call it by many other names such as necessity, time, busy-ness, demands, but all of these can be forms of fear.

Fear produces the most mental, physical and spiritual fatigue that has ever overtaken man. It rushes him so that he has accidents. It drains him of strength to resist illness. It tells him he cannot produce enough to meet the demands upon him. And it builds within his mind such dire images so that he cannot face the simplest.

Fear has one antidote. It is not to stop worrying and take it easy, but it is faith. Adverse conditions cannot break a man in the face of faith. It allows him to look fear in the face with such confidence that it becomes so well known it has no power.

English divine, Frederick William Robertson, wrote, "To believe is strong. Doubt cramps energy. Belief is power."

103

At those times when we have planned for something and have our hearts set on our affairs going in a certain direction but they fail to materialize, we are disappointed. If we have any faith at all, we must remember that one door never closes but another opens. That which once seemed the right thing to plan for may not hold all the things that would be for our good in the long run. It may have been right in the beginning, but as time passes and other events come into being, a change may be necessary for the benefit of the over-all picture.

Sometimes we fix our attention so rigidly on one thing, one part of life, one person, that a change throws us into a state of extreme disappointment. But disappointments like all of the emotions can serve to strengthen rather than take away. The attitude with which we face life can determine its outcome.

We can look with woeful eyes on the negative mental attitude and wallow in self-pity, or we can flip the mind to the upper side and let the positive mental attitude bring to us the strength and peace we need.

Disappointment is something no one has escaped. The many plans we make sometimes fade like mist in the sunlight. A cherished dream may take another shape and to lose that vision can throw a dim view on all of life. Because one tiny part could not be fulfilled, we are so tempted to let all of the rest go with it.

But if only we could wait a bit! So often we then come to realize the reason for our change in plans.

Sometimes disappointment is the very thing that keeps us mounting the steps upward, keeps us stretching our minds to understand. And it may test our spirits. For if disappointment can make a spirit bitter, the joy of accomplishment would have soon soured.

There's no gaiety to a disappointment, but it may be the thing to save us from a life of mediocrity.

English novelist Edward George Bulwer-Lytton wrote, "Man

must be disappointed with the lesser things in life before he can comprehend the full value of the greater."

⊱Isn't it true that when someone says something is wrong, our first thought is "What have I done wrong now?" That constant fear of having a finger of accusation pointed in our direction—that guilt complex that can plague a person into admitting guilt when it isn't even his.

Shakespeare wrote, "The mind of guilt is full of scorpions." And surely it is. For we often take more on with a feeling of guilt than is required of us. It is more often only a feeling of fear, fear of being ridiculed, blamed or even threatened.

A guilt complex can be erased. Not in a day, and maybe not completely, unless we are dedicated to keeping it out of our minds. We are so prone to throw fuel on the fire that we must always be completely aware of the thoughts we entertain.

But certainly, with turning to our innate faith and wisdom we can find enough courage to recognize the ghosts of guilt and see them for what they are.

Perhaps in the final analysis we find we were not guilty at all. We feel relieved, but if we were guilty, the relief of admitting mistakes is just as great.

⊱It has become increasingly noticeable how the "power grab" has reached even the lower levels of living. It is a right thing for man to try to raise himself. To fail to try would earmark him for failure . . . and yet up the shaky ladder of success climb so many bodies without spirits, so little understanding of what is ahead . . . and often less of what is past.

If man could only realize his power comes not from grasping the coattails of others, but from a higher source that knows the way . . . that places before him the right steps, the correct manner, the much needed wisdom and inspiration.

Why is it that when all this guidance is available to man, he lets the littleness of his soul hold him back, believing all the time that any forward motion is because he has learned how to twist situations to his own avail.

How sad the lot of he who discovers all the rungs on his ladder are on the same level. "Power will intoxicate the best hearts, as wine the strongest heads," wrote Caleb Colton, an eighteenth-century clergyman. "No man is wise enough, nor good enough, to be trusted with unlimited power."

Each of us know that if it were not for the little kindnesses, the helping hands that we receive from those who touch our lives daily, we would fall more often and much harder. Yet, we must remember there comes a time when we cannot expect others to rush to our aid. It is then that we test the strength of our own self reliance.

We should make every effort to be worthy of the concern and help of others. It is in sharing all phases of life that makes living more than just an existence. But no one can support a person for long who has no will to use his self reliance. It is said that God helps those who help themselves, but even God cannot help where help is refused.

Then, how much can we depend on ourselves? How would we react to the same situations we see other people experiencing daily? We, who depend so much on our external advantages to pull us through, cannot truthfully foretell our actions in a crisis. But we can have a reserve of faith and strength behind us so that when others reach out to lift us up, we shall be worthy of their time spent in helping to build our self reliance.

In those moments when a quiet man sits with mind centered on the fact that God is only good, and that no situation devious or twisted in appearance, has any power except that which he gives it by dwelling on how terrible it is—then, there is hope.

If that man can become quiet enough in his own mind to know God is good, it will produce one of those times of sweet serenity that settles like an invisible veil between him and his troubles. In those moments of growth and faith will come peace that passes all understanding.

It is good to live an active life, but some of life's most productive moments are not when the mind and body are hurled through hectic hours at a furious pace. Life offers many tender and beautiful times that demand nothing and give only a quiet calm that will never come in pill form.

Contrary to the belief in any power except God's, there is a happy medium. It does not come simply by demanding, and there are times when it can be touched on only so briefly. But even in man's sore travail there is a time when life finds balance and he lives in harmony with God's laws.

It is easy to have faith in God and love everyone on days when the world is all in order.

There are other days that seem to require more effort than any normal person can possibly muster. Each step seems to be an obstacle to overcome. Every hurt and thought of resentment presents itself in a clamorous roar.

Weariness of body, soul and spirit will nag the strongest being into a dark mood unless he can find a time away from all that has plagued him. That time may be hard to come by, but even a few moments can bring our problem to light.

Twinges of jealousy, feelings of anxiety, all scatter in that light. When the attention is turned from those things that make life all too ordinary they immediately, like a procession, march toward the God-self.

To spend only a few moments counting our blessings will tell us that life is well worth living . . . the satisfaction of a job well done, the companionship of good friends with whom we share the lighter side and the ones who understand even in our darkest moods are all blessings.

Everyone must have a way of life. The home, the position, the social level, the health of the body and of the emotions are all a part of daily living. But beyond that there must be a reason, a way of life. We must believe in something, live by something and have a shelter within ourselves where there are no pretenses.

Life cannot be one gay round of living on the surface. It is a thing of depth and width and height, and full of avenues never investigated. Like the body, it is made up of many parts. Beneath the skin there must beat a heart, a network of nerves, the strength of muscles, and much we cannot begin to explain.

As the body depends upon the heart we must have in our lives something to depend upon, something with which to identify ourselves. There must be a central point, a hitching post to keep all of life running smoothly.

We need something to help us retreat as well as to go forward. We must have something to live by, as well as something for which we would willingly die. We need divine wisdom to see, and the strength to break away, those almost invisible fingers of possessiveness that grip our lives.

We do not simply live, we live because. We live because of others, because of beautiful things and times and places. We live because God gave us life, to be happy in, and to find a special way.

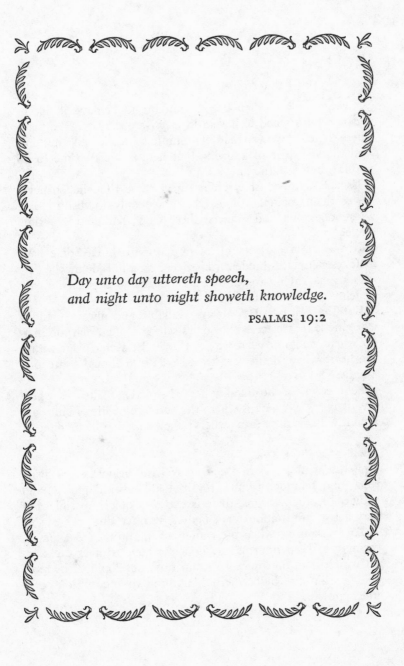

*Day unto day uttereth speech,
and night unto night showeth knowledge.*

PSALMS 19:2

Every so often when there's thinking to be done it does a person a lot of good to have a little private retreat . . . a place where there's no worry that any minute someone will interrupt. And the very ease of knowing that here is a little time to do nothing but just think.

Except that I must carefully direct those thoughts so never to let them roam to things that serve only to disturb. But where does one find a place these days that affords a time alone?

It doesn't take an awful lot of room to think. Some have little special places hidden from view . . . a hillside maybe . . . a sunny spot along a path . . . a closet not so large . . . a park bench . . . or even to take a drive.

But the place that is always available and always used by everyone is that place within one's self. It is here that, no matter where we go or what we do, this is the secret place within the heart where desires are stored . . . and thoughts are productive.

Here is where the thankfulness is stored . . . here is where love is born . . . here is where the very life of life is built and rebuilt. This is my retreat when there's thinking to be done.

When winter presses a cold, gray hand against every living thing and temporarily puts to sleep all outward growth and activity of other seasons, there is within a quiet, invisible, but very active preparation for a lighter, warmer time.

There are times when the winters of life press hard upon us, seeming to keep from us any hope for good. But as the coldest winter does not prevent a tulip from developing a blaze of color within the bulb, there is nothing to prevent our own inner growth.

We quite naturally want the things that will make us happy and we want them now. But there is still a time of preparation, the development of our abilities to recognize the good and the beautiful when we see it. Otherwise, we are apt to look past them, still searching.

The tulip has a plan drawn by God's hand, and more beautiful than anything man could create. We have a way of moving from one time to another, waiting for life to come to us instead of having a plan. But during those waiting periods we need to make a little effort to determine the course and to be ready when the right time comes.

It is said that pearls worn by a happy person have a warm and more lustrous glow.

Pearls are like gentle moments strung together for the happy person—they cannot help but glow.

Gentle moments, like pearls, seem to be so few. Yet, how rich and warm and beautiful they make our lives.

It takes only a few moments to enjoy a talk with someone about good things instead of the bad; it takes only a few moments to drop a line to a shut-in when attention means so much. It takes only a few moments to see a sunset, or read a Scripture, or listen to a child talk.

It takes only a few moments to open the door to happiness. And if happiness seems only a few moments long, so will trouble if we open the door and let it out instead of harboring it.

Life is made up of a few moments all strung together like pearls. Each moment is a pearl, and it is up to us to pick the ones with the highest lustre. If we do not have time to do great things, take a few gentle moments and do small things in a great way.

Some of the dearest moments ever spent are those on the road I didn't want to travel. And some of the most magnificent doors I've ever passed through are where before there was no way.

Some of the kindest people I shall ever know are the ones I didn't want to meet. And the greatest abundance I've ever received came from a pittance I wanted to withhold.

Tears I have wanted to shed have turned to happiness because for a moment I could see beyond them. And hope has saved everything when I wanted most to give up in despair.

And suddenly I realize how great my progress could be if only I could get myself and my emotions out of the way. How hard I push against the door that opens inward—inward, where faith and hope and trust abide.

There's not enough ambling done any more. There are too many deadlines. Time for a favorite TV show, time to take pills, time for appointments, time to catch a plane. Life is one continual alarm clock.

Never a gentle gait, but always at a dogtrot to meet those deadlines. It seems that dawdling along or staring into space is a waste of time, as the ambitious, eager for superiority, move dangerously ahead.

Many great men have known the wisdom of safeguarding their health and security by taking time to analyze, not in the role of fact sifting, but by allowing the mind to amble, to drift openly from thought to thought. This sitting idly on the sidelines and fishing quietly in the mind can catch many a solution that casting would never hook.

After a period of creative silence, attacking any deadline is made more simple. The mind has had time to lay down the brittle aggressiveness and is ready to operate efficiently. Even physical weariness passes and the goal ahead isn't so far in the distance.

When there isn't time to go fishing, remember the words of American author William Mathews: "Knowledge is acquired by study and observation, but wisdom cometh by opportunity of leisure. The ripest thoughts come from a mind which is not always on the stretch, but fed, at times, by a wise passiveness."

Some of my most productive moments are not when I consider how evil the world is, but how powerful is my God.

Some of the best times are not all when I'm enjoying life, but when those I love are knowing happiness.

The highest peak of wealth comes when the joy within surpasses anything I can create out here.

The bloom of good health is felt more richly when I let it flow through me rather than dwelling on the possibility of sickness.

Friendships are strongest and most true when I don't worry about giving more than I receive.

In order that others forgive me, I must also learn to forgive.

I must never forget that negative thoughts feed on fear and starve on faith.

One of the greatest mistakes I can make is to believe myself to be without friend or faith or opportunity.

These personal proverbs belong to every thinking person who wants his life to have more meaning, know more happiness and feel more richly the love that is the medicine for the sickness of the world.

I don't know what time it is. It may be very late,
But I have dreams to dream and thoughts to think that simply
    cannot wait.
I don't know what the weather is, it may be sun or snow.
But in these books and at this time are things I need to know.
I'm not so sure that I'm alone, or if there's someone there;
It would be nice to hear a voice, for there is much to share.
I don't need to know your faults, they may not be for me.
No critic enters in this place, nor do my faults they see,
For only One Pure Being knows the time, or shows through
    your dear face,
Only the One Presence fills our hearts to share this quiet place.

Autumn, described by John Keats as the season of mists and mellow fruitfulness, is the most restful of all seasons. Man is so sensitive to a change of seasons. And at this particular time he stops to consider what his harvest is, and then the age-old promise to himself that next year will be better, and more productive.

But now the peace and serenity of the season is upon him, and the Artist has painted for his eyes to see the most beautiful of all seasons—the autumn.

Scattered frost has touched everything just enough to give a mottled pattern of brown and green. Early morning mists, blue and gray, hang low in the hills; brilliant red sumac and maples gold and burgundy stand out like jewels among the yellow elms.

There is a whole new world for those who wish to open their spiritual eyes. We need to insist that worries take the back seat while we sniff the sweet scent of wood smoke, and see the lavender-pink sunsets and autumn haze that settles like soft, blue fingers through the valleys. This is a picture for the soul by the Master Artist!

Why is it that we require so much scientific proof for the most ordinary things these days, when the very fact that we lie down and close our eyes at night is the highest proof that God's world is in order. Though perhaps our personal world may not know such sequence. There comes a time when our human limitations insist that we lay down our questions and accept by faith the only way to survive ourselves.

To those who say they must have tangible evidence, that the world and all its wonders be displayed before their eyes to see in wisdom the way things really are. And yet who said the human eyes could see or ears could hear more than one tiny bit of the wonder. Who could be so bold as to believe his senses were strong enough to know, except through faith.

Who could see with the visible eye the hand that changes the seasons, or hear Job's stars that sang together at dawn. Who sets the day at rest and brings the morning in all its newness.

Only so far . . . then explanations know no more . . . and though we try to disbelieve when all goes wrong, there comes a time when we want no more explanation than that God's world is in order—and man cannot change it.

Surely if someone took our hand and asked us to come walk along the world and view the wonders so magnificently displayed. . . . If by some miracle we could see the vastness of it all at once, and still bear up under the beauty of it. . . .

If we could see the rolling rise and fall of the land—the purple, pink and golden hues of shadows hung along the mountain sides. . . . If our ears could hear the music of the rippling streams, the rushing waters, the graceful falls.

If by some mere chance we could sense the ebb and flow, the push and relaxing of the tides, the rise and set of the sun, the glittering stars and soft-faced moon that ignores the fact that other worlds encircle ours. . . .

And as the seasons sprinkle rain and flowers, golden leaves and snowfall. . . . On this continuous circle . . . always new . . . always beautiful. . . .

If we can see all this, how then, can we doubt that here the world that God created and saw as good is good. This is our land, and only man's forgetfulness of its source can make it different.

Your customs and mine may be different at Christmastime. But there is one thing we definitely have in common—the Christ child. Christmas comes to the earth weeks before the great day. Those who are aware will see the signs and rejoice. For very early in an autumn morning when the earth is still in darkness, it seems to shrink to a very small size, and the sky is infinitely deep and crystal clear. And in that very early morning sky one brilliant star hangs like a jewel in illuminated silence. How moving and beautiful. One can almost expect to see the Wise Men silhouetted against the horizon—and see the manger.

It is a vision to look for in the pre-Christmas season, more beautiful than all of art, more beautiful than all the world's grandeur. And it is there for those who wish to rise and look —but, then, so is the Christ.

115

There is an old Arabian proverb that if you pitch a lucky man in the Nile he will come up with a fish in his mouth. Just to come up would be enough for most of us, but still we do so many things—perhaps half in jest—that we have hopes will throw off the evil spirits and bring good luck to the rescue.

The tokens we carry we've carried from childhood, when we were careful never to step on a crack in the walk, or pick up a pin—the silly poems that fascinate children, and sometimes follow them into adulthood when the laughter is gone.

What is a lucky man? He's really someone who can rise with the sun letting yesterday go . . . and feel within his heart the gratitude of being alive . . . to have the opportunity to glean from his mistakes something that will take him far over that place if he passes it again. He knows that luck must have a P before it to keep him from waiting, to help him turn up something rather than waiting for something to turn up.

And yes, he's a lucky man who has love to give and has the ability to receive it. He has faith in good. And no small amount of peace when he thinks not how lucky he is, but how blessed!

F